The Sprites and Midgets

To Craig

The Sprites and Midgets

A collector's guide
by Eric Dymock

MOTOR RACING PUBLICATIONS LTD
Unit 6, The Pilton Estate, 46 Pitlake, Croydon CR0 3RY, England

ISBN 0 900549 53 X
First published 1981
Reprinted 1989

Photosetting by Zee Creative Ltd., London SW16
Printed in Great Britain by The Amadeus Press Ltd.,
Huddersfield, West Yorkshire HD2 1YJ

Contents

Introduction

There are cars which inspire respect and there are cars which demand it. There are cars which inspire awe and there are cars which deserve it. There are cars which remain unloved and cars which invite derision. But a few earn something special. Perhaps because they are relatively cheap and likely to crop up in the early years of a motoring lifetime, because they display special qualities of performance or handling, or perhaps through a reputation for strength and reliability, or even because they tend to be used purely for pleasure, some cars inspire real affection.

The Austin-Healey Sprites and MG Midgets, whose production spanned the 21 years between 1958 and 1979, were cars on which successive generations of (mostly) young drivers learned the feel of a sensitive, responsive, small sports car. They were cars on which the impecunious and the enthusiastic could work without tears, or too many special tools. They were cars which could be bought cheaply and run for next to nothing. They were cars upon which even the ungenerous insurance companies would sometimes look kindly because they were never so fast as to constitute an unacceptable risk.

Above all, the Spridgets, as they affectionately came to be called when the British Motor Corporation's 'badge engineers' adopted the successful Austin-Healey Sprite as the basis for a new MG Midget, had the elusive quality of charm. From the pert, chubby looks of the Mark I 'frog-eyed' Sprite, through the better proportions of its restyled replacement, to the relatively unlovely but practical soft-faced cars after 1974, they generated warm feelings and justifiable popularity.

Drivers liked them in their heyday for their precise, taut feel, their sensitive steering, their liveliness and their economy. Passengers may have been lukewarm about the firm ride — perhaps sometimes anxious over the enthusiasm of the driver. Yet parents tended to look on Spridgets as safer than most sports cars; certainly they had no real vices, or unexpected characteristics with which to trap the inexperienced or the unwary. But they could be driven astonishingly quickly by the skilled, and drivers of bigger sports cars looked on them with derision only when the road was straight and long.

The Spridget could be derided by the sporty set, following the advent of the Mini-Cooper, or the faster versions of fairly mundane cars such as the Ford Escort. It very quickly became demodé for racing. With the appearance of small, mid-engined swankpots such as the Fiat X1/9 it was frankly outclassed. When rallies became really rough-and-tumble affairs, decided on forest special stages, the Spridget was too low, too slow and probably too fragile.

Yet rarely has a major car manufacturer lent his name (or even a part of it) to a car so manageable, so responsive and such fun. Alas, the same great Corporation discontinued it, just as it was coming of age. It will thus retain the Peter Pan-like quality of never having quite grown up.

Yet, in a different economic climate from that optimistic age into which the Sprite was launched, its place is somehow more secure than ever. There remain generations of young drivers who look for exactly the characteristics of fun and sensibility that the Spridget provides. There remain generations of older drivers who enjoy recapturing the spirit of youth and vigour of the little cars at a price they can still afford. Austin-Healey Sprites and MG Midgets are likely to remain the bargain-basement classics for as long as they survive in large numbers — and for as long as there are drivers devoted to their health and welfare.

This book is for these drivers.

But it is also for anyone who has admired the sprightliness of the little cars that were the inheritors of a tradition laid down by Cecil Kimber in the 1920s. The idea of a cheap sports car based on the mechanical components of an ordinary family car may not have been his alone, but with the MG he showed how to do it well, if not especially profitably, and survive.

It took the redoubtable Healey family to show MG how it should be done in the 1950s, for which they were ungenerously treated following the Leyland takeover. In British motor industry terms, the Spridget was probably the apogee of the cheap sports car movement, which had traditionally made its home in the Midlands since Kimber's time, but went into decline, together with many other components of the domestic motor industry, with the changing demands and economic realities of the crisis-laden 1970s.

Who knows how many Spridgets survive in the world? With no more being made, their rate of attenuation will diminish as they become more cherished with the passing years.

'Best Buys' in Sprites and Midgets remain fruitful sources of debate. Was the Mark I Sprite too quick and nervous, or the post-1974 Midget overweight and soggy? Do the makers deserve credit for making the thing at all, or obloquy for despoiling and discarding it? Either way, there is a huge reserve of Sprites and Midgets which will continue to give lively, economical and safe service for many years to come, an important link in the chain of motoring archaeology to the days when cars were neither designed with the aid of computers, nor built with the help of robots.

They were made by men with an intuitive feel for engineering, at a time when enterprise was still an important ingredient for success in the motor industry.

August 1981   ERIC DYMOCK

Acknowledgements

Anders Clausager, of BL Heritage, is acknowledged elsewhere for his help in compiling the tables and charting the production history of Sprites and Midgets, but that is no excuse for overlooking the assistance he also provided in obtaining photographs from the archives at Cowley and checking over a number of other mysteries concerning the cars. My thanks also go to Anders for arranging for me to photograph BL Heritage's MG Midget, the last in the long, happy line, together with the matchless Mark I Sprite belonging to Jim Rose, of Safir Engineering. Jim also provided much useful advice on the restoration of Sprites in general, and Mark Is in particular, his own car leaving no doubt about his expertize on the subject.

Nobody would presume to write about Healeys of any sort without talking to the family, and Geoffrey Healey not only wrote three of the standard works on the subject, *Healey: The Specials*, *Austin-Healey* and *More Healeys*, published by Gentry Books, but he also very kindly read the proofs of this book, correcting a number of matters of fact and putting me right on some conclusions I had drawn incorrectly. Acknowledgement to all the Healeys goes almost without saying — without them there would have been no car to write a book about.

My thanks are also due to Ray Hutton, editor of *Autocar*, for allowing me access to his magazine's photographic files, and for permission to publish a number of pictures taken by *Autocar* staff photographers over the years, particularly those on rallies, which were the work of Ron Easton.

Needless to say, many more people deserve acknowledgement for having helped, answered questions and provided material for this book over many years — from the man who sold me my first Sprite well over two decades ago. To them all, my grateful thanks.

Finally, an explanation. In dedicating *The Sprites and Midgets* to my son Craig, I should like to express the hope that he and his generation enjoy the same happy, economical and, above all, safe motoring with sensitive, rewarding and exciting small cars as I and my generation did with Sprites.

                                                                                                      ERIC DYMOCK

The Austin-Healey Sprite at the time of its launch, in May 1958. This left-hand-drive car reveals the windscreen in its original form, with a row of press-studs along the top edge.

CHAPTER 1

Ancestors and parentage

Austin, Morris and the Healey connection

The line of descent of the Austin-Healey Sprite is easily established. The Austin-Healey 100, and its derivative 100-Six and 3000, provided the background and established the connection between the Healey family and the British Motor Corporation. The Austin A30 and A35 and the Morris Minor 1000 provided the mechanical components for a small sports car, in the same fashion as Morris had provided the wherewithal for MGs between the wars.

The abrasive Sir Leonoard Lord, who had led Austin into the merger with Morris to form the British Motor Corporation in 1952, had already identified the market for a small sports car. The year following the amalgamation, the Austin Drawing Office at Longbridge worked on the general arrangement of a replacement for the prewar Austin Seven Nippy and Ulster. The proposal was for a tubular-framed two-seater, using components from, and bearing a superficial resemblance to, the Austin A30, which had been introduced in 1951.

It was too far removed from the production car ever to get off the drawing board, and remained one of the secret projects which car makers reel off, ready to exploit should the market demand it. The Austin-Healey partnership was already under way, with the superbly styled Austin-Healey 100, introduced at the Earls Court Motor Show in the autumn of 1952.

Lord had preferred the Healey to the 1952 EX 175 prototype proposed by MG. This was the car which would evolve into the MGA of 1955, but it was put into suspended animation for two years, much to the chagrin of the Abingdon factory, where the ageing TF needed a hasty revamp to try and keep up. Lord's antipathy to MG was reputed to stem from an old quarrel with

Lord Nuffield, and led to the supposed short-changing of the non-Austin side of the British Motor Corporation. There was more to it, of course; the Nuffield side was older, and more run-down.

BMC was still a distant prospect when Donald Healey had built his reputation. First, he was a competition driver, later technical director of Triumph where, in charge of design and experimental work, he had been responsible for the Gloria and Dolomite. In 1939, he was promoted to be Triumph's general manager.

With the war over, and Triumph in receivership, Healey began making cars on his own account. He started in a small factory at The Cape, Warwick, using engines from Riley (for whom he had worked before joining Triumph in 1934). The four-cylinder, high-camshaft engines made the hand-built Healeys amongst the fastest cars catalogued in Britain in the late-1940s. Their reputation was enhanced by some well-publicised achievements in the Mille Miglia, and also by record-setting ploys, emphasizing their 100-mph performance. The styling was in the bulbous fashion of the period, and with their famous, if rather extravagant, system of trailing-link independent front suspension, the Healeys handled rather better than their run-of-the-mill rivals, which were mostly designs carried over from 1939.

The Healey sold well in the United States, bolstered by the competition success of the Silverstone model, and in September 1949 Donald Healey struck a bargain with George Mason, of the Nash Kelvinator Corporation. The agreement to build a new sports car, using the 3.8-litre, six-cylinder Nash engine, took Healey into a new dimension. The new car was to enjoy the benefit of Nash's sales-and-service network. The giant American firm had the benefit of the Healey family's experience of

traditional sports cars, and stood to benefit from the success of the Nash-Healey in races such as Le Mans and the Mille Miglia.

In terms of Nash output, the 404 Nash-Healeys made between the middle of 1950 and February 1952 was a trifle. But the principle of co-operation between the tiny specialist firm and the big corporation was established. The benefits to both became apparent; increased turnover for the small, and prestige and a modest profit for the large.

For their domestic-market cars, the days of the Riley engine were numbered. By 1951, the Nash-Healey was in decline, and the Healeys clearly had to think what they were going to do next. Amongst their ploys was to take a design, already shown to Nash, and offer it to BMC.

The car was a classic in the making, the Healey Hundred, and one of the best-loved and best-looking sports cars ever. Austin and Nash were already working on the prototype Nash Metropolitan, so it was commercially appropriate for Donald Healey to incorporate the A90 Atlantic engine and running gear into the design.

Despite the rebuff from Nash, Healey went ahead with a

The 948-cc Austin A35 saloon, which was announced as a successor to the 803-cc A30 in October 1956 and whose engine (shared with the Morris Minor) would soon power the first Austin-Healey Sprite. Publicity at the time spoke of the 'quick-action four-speed gearbox, controlled by a short, sports-car-type gear lever, floor-mounted', which would also find its way into the Sprite, along with the A35's front suspension and rear axle.

There was less to raid from the Morris Minor for the jig-saw which made up the Austin-Healey Sprite. Nevertheless, it bequeathed its matchless rack-and-pinion steering, and its rear-axle ratio of 4.55:1 was also in demand as an alternative to the A35's 4.22:1 ratio.

The Healey family's gift for identifying a timeless style was never better exemplified than in the original Austin-Healey 100, seen here at Sebring, in 1953, with Donald Healey accompanying George Eyston, who was to be instrumental in many of Healey's American record-breaking ploys.

This 1947 prototype MG reached the full-scale mock-up stage. It was a proposal to update the Midget two-seater by the Cowley drawing office and was to have had an overhead-camshaft 1,100-cc engine also destined at the time for the Wolseley Wasp, a stillborn derivative of the Morris range.

prototype. He was convinced he was on the right track, and encouraged by Austin's reaction to a modern all-metal (as opposed to a coachbuilt, wood-frame-bodied) sports car, of a sort which the increasingly valuable United States market would absorb. Healey knew the country. He had been selling cars there for five years, and he sensed the mood of the coming sports car boom.

The arrangement with Nash became the pattern for the one forged with Austin, and the Austin-Healey 100, together with the rival Triumph TR2 introduced in 1953, filled the sports car market at a cheaper price than the brilliant Jaguar XK 120, but above that of the traditional (and slower) MG and Morgan.

The entrepreneurial and engineering skills of the Healey family were at their most vigorous. Donald's experience was backed with the skill and creative talent of his sons, Geoffrey, in charge of technical development, and his younger brother Brian. Together, they built prototypes on their own initiative, keeping their eyes and ears open for opportunities to exploit them. They worked rather like a freelance development department, selling manufacturing rights of designs which they had been alert enough

The Nash-Healey in its 1950 form, based on the Healey Silverstone chassis, modified to accept the six-cylinder 3.8-litre Nash engine. The grille, head-lamps and bumpers are amongst the identifiable Nash items. This car was a precursor of the Austin-Healey in that it showed the way for co-operation between the small, specialist design shop and the large manufacturer with an extensive sales network.

Another MG proposal, which in this instance did not progress beyond the scale-model stage. Note the reversion to a stylized form of traditional MG grille, an idea which was to be carried forward to the forthcoming MG Magnette.

to produce, almost before the big manufacturers realized they were needed.

Some of their projects never saw the light of day, others were stillborn as rolling chassis, but following a conversation with Sir Leonard Lord in 1956, Donald Healey embarked on yet another. He started work on a new, small, low-cost sports car. Although it was years before he realized it, he was working in the idiom of the discarded 7 hp sports tourer of 1953. Its plans remained firmly locked away in the Austin archives, but in any case, Healey had ideas of his own. Amongst *his* archives was a styling scheme drawn up in 1952 by his body designer, Gerry Coker, for an A30-engined sports car.

Lord's remarks may have contained a broad hint. He was looking for a smaller, less powerful alternative to the 100 and the new 100-Six. He wanted a car that would be a little less fierce — his North American dealers had told him that the big Healey's power and speed had put some customers off, and more than three-quarters of those made were being written-off in accidents. They identified a market for a small sports car.

CHAPTER 2

The first Austin-Healey Sprite

Creating a new sports car concept

If there was one capacity which Donald Healey had demonstrated, time and again, during his years in the motor industry it was a well developed 'feel' for the sports car market. Once again, he knew exactly what the public wanted. There was, however, no formal commission. BMC did not pay for a specific design study, although there was already a liaison, and an arrangement for exchanging information with the Healeys. This included Austin making available components with which prototype development could be carried out, and there was even a go-between, Geoff Cooper, who supplied the drawings and specifications of relevant production parts, such as the A35 front suspension, engine and axle.

These were amongst the ingredients for the car Donald Healey had in mind, and they originated in the Austin side of BMC, which was expedient bearing in mind Lord's predispositions. Yet filling the gaps between the proprietary units with the chassis and body of a pert, fast-selling sports car, at a price to suit the market, was something which required flair.

A few changes were inevitable. The A35's mechanically operated rear brakes dangled underneath, reducing ground clearance, but they would have been unsuitable for a sports car in any case, so they were rejected. Likewise, the Cam Gears steering box, with its ball-joints and idler arm, would not have achieved the steering response that was wanted, so a Morris Minor rack-and-pinion was used instead. An MG twin master-cylinder offered the opportunity to actuate the clutch hydraulically, and an MG manifold for the twin SU carburettors, replacing the Austin's single Zenith, found their way into the specification of the prototype.

Once the principal components were fixed, design work began on a layout which might have been inspired by the D-Type Jaguar, Britain's premier sports car. At the time, Britain was sweeping the board at Le Mans, and gaining great prestige for the motor industry in the European Economic Community then being established. The main feature of the D-Type was a stiff centre structure, enclosing the cockpit and scuttle, with the engine and front suspension on outriggers at the front. The rear axle was trailed along, feeding all its loads into the centre portion, rather than the tail of the car, which accordingly could be built as an extremely lightweight shell.

Jaguar adopted a similar pattern for the 2.4 saloon, in which the rear suspension loads were also cantilevered into the centre-section of the car. The D-Type's middle was a magnesium monocoque, but for their brainchild, the Healeys chose a simple platform which effectively terminated just behind the seats. Stiffness was provided by the deep, enclosed propeller-shaft tunnel, which joined with the scuttle pressings at the front, and the sloping, transverse panel at the rear, just forward of the axle.

The door sills were 5 in (12.7 cm) deep, fully boxed, and longitudinal-section pressings were welded to the floor underneath the seats. At the rear of the platform, these represented the take-up points for the suspension, and at the front they met a beam running the width of the car, roughly under the driver's knees. This formed the main cross spar on which the scuttle structure and the front longitudinals were mounted.

The engine and front suspension sat on these outriggers once again (easily manufactured top-hat-section beams) and the scuttle was built up around the firewall bulkhead, which enclosed the

The original Sprite in profile. The clean lines of this model relied on good proportions to provide the eye-appeal so important to sports car buyers. The front bumper was optional, and only overriders were provided at the rear. Lucas supplied the same tail-lights to the Triumph TR2.

A Sprite with a difference or two. A hardtop and a discreet 'Twin-Cam' badge above the rear numberplate were identification features of the author's second Mark I. The fashionable Michelin X tyres tended to over-fill the wheelarches.

Right-side view of the Austin-badged engine as used in the original Sprite. Note how the coil is strapped securely on top of the dynamo, which has a reduction gearbox to the rear for driving the tachometer, when fitted.

footwells. The bulkhead fabrication carried forward extensions, which formed the inside front wings, very basic mudguards which did no more than keep the worst of the splashes off the engine.

All panels were kept as simple as possible; most were flat, and the only double-curvatures were in the body pressings. Those welded to the platform, and making up the tail of the car, formed a hollow shell, very light through being relatively unstressed, and gaining strength through not having a boot aperture. Luggage space was generous, but it was reached through the yawning, cave-like mouth behind the seats.

A one-piece bonnet was not entirely a new idea. It had been a feature of sports cars such as the DB2 Aston Martin, and the Lotus 11, to say nothing of the D-Type. These hinged forward, but this arrangement proved impractical for the new small car,

whose owners would long remember the muddy handle and the hearty heave it took to lift the entire structure, complete with grille and headlights, on to the ratchets of the supporting struts. It gave unparalleled accessibility to the drum brakes, front suspension and steering rack. It even made the engine fairly easy to get at, but it left the battery in a dark region at the back, and topping-up was a job for the agile, best left until the engine was cool.

The body was a masterpiece of simplicity and practicality, although Coker's 1952 ideas had proved too expensive to consider. There was very little to it, once the platform and scuttle had been designed. The proportions more or less spoke for themselves, but several schemes were drawn up and rejected nonetheless, including one in which the front and rear pressings were identical for ease of manufacture. Panel Craft of

The same engine from the left side. The mechanical fuel pump was never easy to reach beneath the carburettor heat shield, while the pancake air filters were the source of a certain amount of intake noise.

Birmingham turned out two prototypes once Gerry Coker had developed his drawings to full-size, on a board 20 ft × 6 ft, from which a body buck was made.

The shape of the prototype was essentially that of the production car. In an effort to keep costs down, external hinges were used for the bonnet and doors, on the lines of the Wilmot-Breeden hinges used on the boot-lids of the big Healeys. The first prototype had pop-up headlights operated by a linkage of rods and levers, but this was abandoned in view of the expense and complication.

The floor pan and the scuttle, the front suspension and the location of the major components survived throughout the model's 21-year history. However, the body changed, and notwithstanding its importance as a feature of the original design, so did the rear suspension.

Each quarter-elliptic spring was composed of 15 leaves, with the master leaf carried round to form the spring eye. There was also a reinforcing part-length leaf secured by spring clips. Location of the axle was by uprights, welded to the casing inboard of the wheels. The springs were bushed to the bottom of the uprights, and torque reaction arms attached to the top. These trailed from the rear bulkhead and were a simple metal pressing with Metalastik bushes. The original design ran the torque reaction arms and the arm of the lever-type dampers together, but severe local stressing showed up on the first batch of cars, and the arms were repositioned to act on two more brackets, inboard of the uprights.

John Thompson Motor Pressings already made the chassis-frames for the big Healeys, and after the drawings for the 55 separate parts of the prototype's underframe were completed,

A Mark I engine installed with, judging by the inner wing in the background, the prototype body still incomplete. The casing to the rear of the engine is the heating matrix and the valve immediately ahead of it controls the water supply. The radiator filler cap is on an extension of the header tank in order to keep down the bonnet height.

The Mark I front suspension and drum brake asembly. Although there was an easy path for cooling air to reach the brakes, the drums were undersized, and the later disc brakes were to become a much welcomed development.

they turned out two complete examples within the space of six weeks. The cars were given the designation 'Q', not for the sake of anonymity or secrecy, but simply because it happened to be the next letter in the Healeys' chassis-number book. In due course, complete with the Panel Craft bodies, Q1 and Q2 took to the road for a test-and-development programme, which showed up surprisingly few problems. Q2 had a slightly wider cockpit, and the distinctive frog-eyed headlamps replaced the swing-back ones. Concealed door hinges turned out cheaper after all, and BMC Engineering specified thinner-gauge metal for the body sills, the inner wings and a number of body panels in the interests of cheapness and weight-saving. Lucas wired the cars with a very

straightforward loom, once again keeping the cost down, and they co-operated with Smiths Instruments to provide a novel and cheap means of driving the (optional) tachometer by means of a take-off from the back of the dynamo. The oil pump at the rear of the A35 engine's camshaft precluded a conventional tachometer drive. A gearbox on the dynamo, with a suitable ratio to drive the instrument at engine speed, not only served the purpose, but had the useful side-effect of giving early warning of slack or broken fan belts whenever the rev-counter failed to keep up with the engine. A subsequent service problem with the gearboxes was traced to over-tightening of the nut holding them to the dynamo.

Engine development was carried out by Morris Engines, at

Courthouse Green, Coventry, under Eddie Maher. The increase in power over the A35 was fairly modest at first, although the Morris Minor version already gave 37 bhp on its SU carburettor. Two SU H1 carburettors of 1⅛-in throat diameter raised the output from 34 bhp at 4,750 rpm to 43 bhp at 5,200 rpm, but stronger valve springs, stellite-faced exhaust valves, and copper-lead main as well as big-end bearings held out the promise of better things to come. The compression ratio remained at 8.3:1 for the first, or 9C engine, but flat-topped pistons, as fitted to the 1961 9CG engine, were available to raise the compression to over 9:1.

The 6¼-in Borg and Beck single-dry-plate clutch was provided with stronger springs and, a bonus from using the MG twin cylinder, it was actuated hydraulically. The A35 gearbox retained

The Mark I Sprite from beneath. Difficulties with installing the engine and gearbox from underneath precluded assembly of the car on the A35 line at Longbridge. Quarter-elliptic springs suspend the axle from the rear of the ribbed part of the floor platform.

its standard, rather wide ratios, and the axle ratio remained at 4.22:1. It was not long before enthusiasts discovered that alternatives were available, ranging from the 3.727:1 of the early Riley 1.5, through the 3.9:1 which BMC Competitions made available, to the 4.55:1 of the Morris Minor, the 4.375:1 of the A35 van, and the 'tall' 5.3:1 made for the GPO Minor 1000 van. Morris Engines also developed a close-ratio gearbox, which was available to special order.

Testing and development work on the prototypes was interrupted briefly when Donald Healey took Q1 to Longbridge to show it to BMC's Deputy Chairman, George Harriman. Sir Leonard Lord was handing over some responsibilities pending his semi-retirement, and Harriman was made managing director and deputy chairman in 1956, having been production manager at Austin since 1944. It would fall to Harriman to take the decision on the future of the new car, so Healey presented it to him on January 31, 1957. Sir Leonard was to remain group chairman until 1961, so back the car came for his approval as well, on February 20.

With a planned basic price of £450, the type number AN 5, and the Austin Drawing Office (ADO) project number 13, it was decided to go ahead. The name coined was Sprite, the choice of Donald Healey. There was no doubt it suited his conception of a small, sprightly, nimble two-seater in the tradition of the Riley Sprite, a sports car based on a TT racer of 1935. The name had been relinquished to Daimler, who had used it for a 1.6-litre Lanchester in 1956, of which only a handful were built — the last car, as it turned out, ever to bear the distinguished Lanchester name. Healey established that 'Sprite' was available, and BMC secured it.

Production was planned for the A35 line at Longbridge, but this would have entailed a redesign. It was necessary to install the engine and transmission from underneath, but the enclosed transmission tunnel of the Sprite, which contributed so greatly to beam stiffness, prevented this. Major alterations to the engine bay and the front of the chassis would have been needed, so the plan was scrapped, and assembly was assigned to the MG works at Abingdon.

In any case, the A35 line was due to stop, as BMC began gearing-up for the Mini. This would also keep Austin's engine plant very busy, so Sprite engine work was directed to Morris Engines. Moving to Abingdon could have been a source of difficulty, remembering that the Austin-Healey 100 had thwarted MG's plans to introduce the MGA in 1952. Fortunately, John Thornley, MG's managing director, recognized the advantages for his plant and his workforce, who were as keen as he was on the MG reputation. The Sprite was, after all, quite in keeping with MG traditions, and despite the absence of an octagon badge it was accepted cheerfully. In any case, since badge engineering was already a way of life at BMC, an MG version must have seemed a logical corollary in the future. MG already made non-MGs; the Sprite replaced the Riley on the Abingdon line.

Sprite production was never going to reach the numbers that would qualify it for what we should nowadays call economies of scale. It would necessarily be a dispersed operation, entailing much to-ing and fro-ing of components and assemblies on the backs of lorries. It was not a case of muddled planning, an

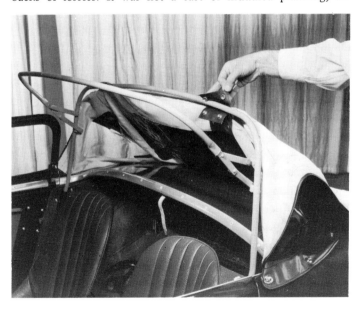

The Sprite's hood irons were completely detachable, and when erected the hood was secured by fasteners which helped to prevent it from flapping at speed.

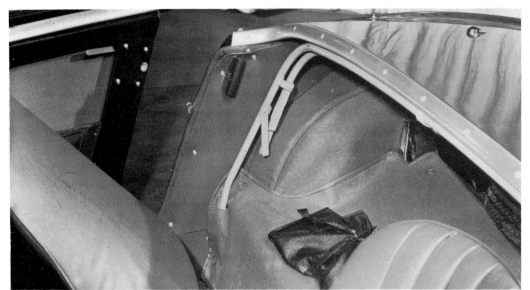

The hood-stowage process. Once the tubular hood framing was removed it could be folded, then reversed, slipped into small pockets in the floor covering and eased back beneath the rear of the cockpit.

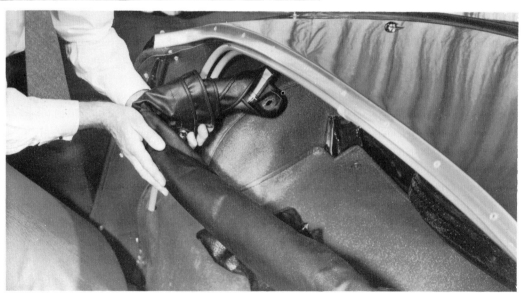

Here the hood fabric has been folded, with the quarter-windows tucked under, so that it can be slipped into the arch of the boot opening.

Two webbing straps were provided to hold the folded hood fabric in place. A large plastic bag was provided for the tool kit. The two chromed buttons on the rear deck were for securing the rear panel of the erected hood.

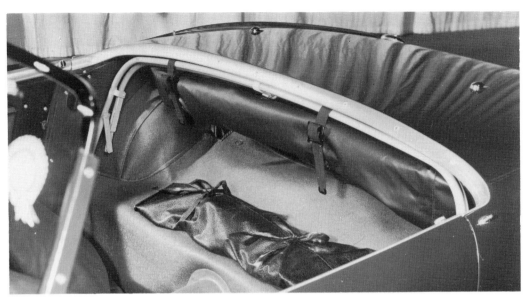

One of the first modifications to the Mark I Sprite was a new means of fixing the front of the hood. A slot in the top windscreen rail accepted a metal bar sewn into the hood fabric, forming an effective, waterproof seal.

ingredient in the later atrophy of the British car industry. It was simply the way things were done at a time when fuel was cheap and production facilities scattered.

The chassis were produced by John Thompson Motor Pressings, of Wolverhampton, who had made the prototype. They were then taken to Swindon, some 75 miles by road, where the Pressed Steel Company produced and welded-on the body panels. The painting was done at the Morris paint shop in Cowley, a distance of some 30 miles, from whence the bodies then made the relatively short trip to Abingdon for trimming and finishing. There, they were joined by the engines and transmissions, following their journey from Coventry.

Owing to the relatively low volume of Sprite production, the waste was largely balanced out by the savings. There was no large investment in integrated plant, and no heavy interest to pay on capital machinery.

The pre-production prototypes showed up the weakness around the rear-suspension attachments, resulting in the modification to the torque link and shock absorber. The body sills buckled on test, so the gauge of the metal was restored from 0.036 in (0.914 mm) to 0.048 in (1.22 mm), which was more or less what the Healeys had recommended in the first place.

Although Geoffrey was a formally trained engineer, and Donald's experience in the motor industry was immense, their engineering tended to be of the instinctive sort. It was appropriate to the times, however, and depended a good deal on the services

Roomy door pockets provided all the pre-winding-window cars with extra elbow room. The earliest door handles had no button, and the inner door skin was ribbed rubber, like the floor. Internal hinges replaced the prototype's external variety.

of technicians such as Barry Bilbie, the chassis designer, and Gerry Coker, the body designer, who went to the United States after working on the first general-arrangement drawings of the Sprite. He was replaced by Les Ireland, who had worked with Donald Healey before the war at Triumph.

Yet the car remained essentially the work of the Healeys. The conception was theirs, the broad terms of the design were theirs, and with their agreeable approach they were able to get the best results from the people and firms with whom they worked. The change of heart over the gauge of the body panels only served to show that their feel for the job was, as often as not, about right. Modern, computer-assisted design would probably have come to a different conclusion, and in some respects the Sprite could be termed 'over-engineered'. It was, perhaps, heavier than it need have been, but this was a characteristic which has contributed to its longevity and value for latter-day owners and collectors.

Other obvious virtues which remain true were the low cost, ready availability and reliable nature of the component parts. The motor trade was familiar with the engine, gearbox and axle, there was nothing new about the suspension or brakes, and Austin dealers could stock spares for virtually nothing over and above their customary commitment.

The announcement was fixed for May 20, 1958, with the price estimates coming with astonishing accuracy only £5 over target, at £455 excluding Purchase Tax.

The Sprite arrived in a market which was still expanding. The

Abingdon's 50,000th sports car coincided with the second year of Mark I Sprite production. The display board was attached, appropriately enough, to an MGA, but the Sprite and the Austin-Healey 100-Six alongside it were a reminder that the factory was now only building sports cars; Riley production had been transferred elsewhere and the MG Magnette ZB saloon had been discontinued.

United Kingdom made a million cars for the first time in 1958, and domestic registrations accounted for 566,000. Imports were insignificant, but although Purchase Tax had come down from its record 66⅔ per cent in 1951-3 to 50 per cent, new cars remained something of a luxury. The nation's love affair with the car was nevertheless at its most passionate. Pollution had hardly been thought of, and safety was still a matter of avoiding accidents rather than avoiding injury when you had them. The rules of the game still did not include Type Approval.

Economy, however, did matter. The Triumph TR2 had shown that 30 mpg (9.42 litres/100 km) was possible from a sports car, and had also pioneered the notion that good proportions were more important in the styling of small, open two-seaters than elaborate double-curvatures. The Sprite owed a certain amount to the TR's characteristic chunkiness, as well as making the acceptance of bulgy headlights easier. They fulfilled a similar function on the Triumph; they made the body cheaper.

There was, however, no real opposition for the Sprite at £660 including tax. The Healey 100-Six cost £1,227 and the Triumph TR3 £1,050. The MGA was £995 and the Morgan 4/4 with 1,172-cc Ford engine £748. The TR3-engined Morgan Plus-4 cost £969, astonishingly undercutting the Triumph, and the keenest opposition to the Sprite was probably the Lotus Seven in kit form, at £690. It would have been £1,036 with Purchase Tax, but nearly all Lotus cars were still sold as boxes of bits for home assembly, thus not qualifying for the tax imposition. The Berkeley, made by a Biggleswade caravan manufacturer, had a transverse engine and front-wheel drive. Its Excelsior 492-cc three-cylinder two-stroke engine made it a lively car at £650, but neither it, nor the Turner with a BMC A-Type engine at £864, were ever made in anything like the numbers necessary to constitute a threat.

Efforts to keep the Sprite's catalogued price down were nonetheless strenuous. The basic ex-works price of the car included hood, sidescreens, rear overriders, spare wheel and tyre, but little by way of ancillary equipment. The floor covering was fluted rubber, and the specification did not run to luxuries such as fore-and-aft adjustment for the passenger's seat. The curious convention of listing the heater as an optional extra on home market cars was maintained, and the list of options was a long one, on the understanding that the (presumably) youthful owners could improve their car's specification as they were able to afford it.

It was probably easier to talk parents into a £679 car, before letting on that completing it with luxuries such as the front bumper could very quickly add a further £100. When the hardtop became available in 1959, this could reach £150. There was still precious little competition, however, and there was nothing in the same class for liveliness, reliability and fun.

For the time, it even was quite well-equipped. The hood was exceptionally clever. The sticks slotted into notches aft of the doors, and the top, with its huge rear window, was draped over two domed catches on the boot top, and secured with pop-stud fasteners along the top of the windscreen rail. One of the first modifications followed a crop of cracked windscreens and demands for better weather-proofing. Rain quickly found its way down the inside of the screen, and little splashes would attack the occupants at speeds over about 50 mph. A solution was found by stitching a metal strip inside the front flap of the hood, which fitted neatly into a slot along the top of a new windscreen.

Many other changes in the Sprite, and its companion Midget, followed in the next 21 years, yet for the most part the car remained similar in character throughout. It is a tribute to the rectitude of the basic design that much of it was still recognizable in 1979. The disposition of the major components, the chassis platform, the front suspension and steering, the rear axle (although not the rear suspension) and the principal dimensions remained little altered from the bug-eyed froglets that had introduced sports-car motoring to a rising generation more than two decades earlier.

CHAPTER 3

From frog-eyes to squashy bumpers

The development of the Sprite and Midget

Sales of the Mark I Sprite remained buoyant for some three years, but BMC Sales and Marketing decreed that by the spring of 1961 a reskin would be necessary. It is open to debate whether the decline in sales towards the end of 1960 was due to the car's appearance or not. The bulging headlamps were not to everyone's taste, nor was the rather heavy bonnet, and boot access *was* problematical. But shortcomings such as these were probably not to blame for the falling-off in sales from the 1959 peak of 21,566 to 18,665 in 1960.

The decline was more likely due to the condition of the UK market, which was poised for a plunge in 1961 from 820,088 new registrations to 756,054. United Kingdom production tumbled from 1.352 million to 1.003 million, a weekly shortfall of 6,707 vehicles. A miniature recession was under way, and a 10 per cent special surcharge on top of car Purchase Tax from July 1961 did nothing to help matters. Nonetheless, changes were considered necessary, perhaps under the mistaken impression that the problem lay with the car. In fact, the slide was never really halted. Even when the market had recovered, and throughout the following two decades, the 1959 total was matched just once, in 1962, and comfortably exceeded only in 1964, when the combined sales of MG Midgets (11,450) and Sprites (11,157) produced a total of 22,607.

Still, BMC was sensitive to criticisms of the styling and accusations that the car was unsophisticated, so instead of making a virtue out of its novel features, the company insisted upon change. The American notion of planned obsolescence was at its wasteful height, it was considered that the Sprite ought to grow up, and so the Mark II was put in hand.

BMC was probably encouraged in the view that price was not critical by the growth of a substantial Sprite support industry. A number of firms, such as Ashley Laminates, produced glass-reinforced plastic bonnets with more conventionally sited headlamps. The Sprinzel, Sebring, Speedwell and Wilson-Spratt Sprites set a vogue for enhancement kits, and the Healeys themselves discovered a market amongst enthusiasts not only willing and able, but positively anxious to spend relatively large sums of money improving their cars mechanically. The optional equipment available from Warwick, and from BMC's own Special Tuning Department at Abingdon, included Shorrock supercharger kits, a roll-bar kit which had been designed for the car while it was still in the prototype stage, and a number of exhaust systems, which produced a certain amount of extra power and made the car sound very much more potent. The exemplary handling, and the obvious reserves of cornering power, encouraged owners to fit engine conversion kits to exploit the roadholding. Some conversion specialists, alas, were of dubious worth, producing engines which were extremely rough, thoroughly unreliable and short-lived.

Towards the end of Mark I production, Healey also produced a wire-wheel and disc-brake kit, and a stylish hardtop, which was made by Jensen and sold by BMC. This was a solid moulding in glass-reinforced plastic, with a toughened glass rear window.

Concurrently with the Mark II Sprite, an MG version was to be introduced, selling through BMC's old Nuffield dealers, the Sprite having been the responsibility of the Austin dealers. They had been selling MGs and Rileys, so it stood to reason they would be more sports car-minded, which made the sales prospects

The Sprite in its Mark II form. The more simple grille, compared with that of the MG Midget, and the lack of chrome strips down the body sides were evidence that the Austin-Healey version would be the poor relation of the Spridget family.

The chrome body strips identify this as a Midget, equipped in this instance with the optional Ace wheel discs. The sliding sidescreens seen here were one of half a dozen such versions, official or otherwise, to be seen before the introduction of winding windows.

The Healey hardtop was a substantial affair, the curved lines of which blended rather more successfully with those of the Mark I Sprite.

encouraging, to say the least. Mechanically, the cars were to be identical, with trim, badging and decoration establishing the difference. For marketing reasons, the MG was to cost slightly more, so it was given the traditional distinguishing features of a top-of-the-range model, such as the chrome strips down each side and a grille with vertical bars instead of mesh.

The rationale was commercial, in keeping with the BMC policy of making the Riley, Wolseley and MG marques up-market versions of the badge-engineered Austin and Morris models. There is no evidence of a campaign to denigrate or downgrade the Sprite against the Midget, or to diminish the status of the Healeys. They received the same royalty on Midgets as they did

on Sprites, but what they did not foresee, of course, was a day when Sprites might no longer be made.

Life with BMC was not always straightforward for the Healeys. Following a series of meetings, at which they were given the guidelines for the Mark II Sprite and told not to mention the changes to MG, they got down to work. A new front for the car was past the clay mock-up stage when Sydney Enever, MG's chief designer, told them he was working on a new rear and that it would probably be a good idea if they got together.

Enever had re-established a design office at Abingdon late in 1954, when BMC at last realized that the MG TF was reaching the end of its useful life. He had developed his cherished EX 175 (later EX 182) into the MGA and put it into production by the end of 1955.

Following that, he was able to start design studies for what would turn out in 1962 to be the MGB, and devote some time to the Mark II Sprite and MG Midget. Enever had been told about the new front, but was able to evade the departmental secrecy and plan the car as a whole with the Healeys.

One reason for the divided responsibilities lay in the ultimate intention to change the car's rear suspension from quarter-elliptic to half-elliptic springs. The object was to remove what critics had called anything from a nervous twitch to '. . . a slight tendency to weave on the straight at maximum speed' *(Motor)*. So fundamental a change implied a major redesign at the rear. Yet the car's whole philosophy depended on putting all the principal stresses into the centre portion. It was thus logical to entrust the alteration to Enever's design office, and let him work out the complications of an opening boot as well, with a result which bore a family resemblance to the embryo MGB.

The Healeys might have resisted the change, and in any case BMC could always keep its options open, giving them the chance

On its introduction at the end of June 1961, the MG Midget was promoted as the first under-1,000cc MG for 25 years. In its original form it was offered with the twin-carburettor BMC A-Series engine in 9:1 compression form, developing 46.4 bhp at 5,500 rpm, although for certain export markets a compression of 8.3:1 was provided, giving 43 bhp at 5,200 rpm.

Facia of the Mark II (and Mark I) Sprite. The black steering wheel with the familiar lightning motif on the horn boss, a tachometer and speedometer figured in the Healey style, and a different texture for the dashboard covering and upholstery material were distinguishing features of the Sprite, while the grab handle on the passenger's side was a legacy from the days of riding mechanics and two-seater racing cars.

Midget Mark I facia features included a padded roll along the top of the dashboard, which was more a concession to style than to safety as it was too soft to do much good. The coloured steering wheel, more detailed figuring on the instruments, but — curiously — no grab handle were amongst the MG customer's rewards for the extra £20 on the basic price. The MG tachometer read to 7,000 rpm, against the Sprite's 6,000, and the MG instrument had two coloured segments.

By the time the Midget reached production, the floor covering was in a flecked material, the seats had contrasting piping, but passengers still had nothing to hold on to. The starter button is to the left of the tachometer, the switch above the ignition key is for the non-cancelling flashing indicators, then comes the manual push for the screenwash, and on the far left, with a straight cable to the carburettor side of the engine, the choke control.

A factory assembly line view taken during the early days of Sprite Mark II/Midget Mark I production, with MGAs still being made on a line at the far side of the Abingdon shop.

to equip the Midget with half-elliptic springs and a proper boot, while leaving the Sprite in the bargain basement with a lighter and cheaper structure.

In the event, half-elliptics were not introduced with the Mark II Sprite, but were postponed until 1964, when commonality extended to a shared announcement date. As it was, the Mark I Midget was scheduled to appear a full month after the Mark II Sprite.

The Healey's scheme for the new front represented no more than building up the wings and providing an opening bonnet in the conventional manner. Its style followed that of the glass-reinforced-plastic lightweight bonnets, with a broader grille and a fashionable air scoop.

Enever's work on the tail was rather more elaborate. The cockpit opening was enlarged, a bulkhead provided, and although the car was only ½ in longer it had a lockable boot, complete with lid. In terms of cubic footage it was little different, much of the space being taken up by the spare wheel, but in matters of convenience it represented a substantial improvement.

The chassis platform, suspension, brakes and interior layout remained the same as before, but the close-ratio gearbox developed at Abingdon became standard. Engine performance was increased by fitting HS2 instead of H1 carburettors, with 1¼-in instead of 1⅛-in chokes, strengthening the crankshaft and installing a new camshaft with a longer exhaust opening period and increased lift. The inlet valves were enlarged, double valve springs being fitted, and a new exhaust manifold was provided. Along with the hitherto optional 9:1 compression ratio, the changes increased power by a modest 3 bhp, but the stronger crank improved the engine's smoothness, and the extra power

BMC offered this rather angular hardtop for the Mark I Midget, which was more in keeping with the car's tail-end treatment (also adopted for the MGB) than the Healey hardtop with its more rounded profile.

33

With its hood folded and sidescreens removed the MG Midget looked at its best for this publicity shot, taken at Blenheim at the time of its launch in 1961. Perforated disc wheels were still being featured at this stage.

Another view of an early Midget, with sidescreens in place and the hood erect and showing a commendably taut fit.

Not quite such a good fit with this hood, on which the useful quarter-windows can be seen to greatly aid rear-view vision. The upturn in the body sill behind the front wheelarch echoed the lifting bonnet of the Mark I throughout the Spridget's 21-year history.

more than compensated for the extra weight. The new car was 3 mph faster and 3 seconds quicker to 60 mph.

The scooped-out portion of the tail was described as suitable for carrying a third passenger, or children, and a seat cushion was listed amongst the options. Even the publicity pictures were not entirely convincing, however, on this score and the idea of the Sprite being anything but a two-seater was never seriously entertained. Owners tended to look on the space as supplementary luggage accommodation. The change meant that a new means of storing the hood sticks had to be found, so they

were split and consigned to the boot. Otherwise, the very satisfactory hood was the same as before, and sliding Perspex sidescreens, previously available as an option, were standardized. Windscreen washers and, in view of pending legislation, seat-belt anchorages also became standard.

When the Midget appeared at the beginning of July 1961, it had a different type of flecked rubber floor covering, a gold-coloured steering wheel instead of a black one and three hood colours amongst its distinguishing features. The instrument faces had clearer figuring, and the seats contrasting piping, to take

Throughout the life of the Spridget, considerable efforts were made to improve the quality of the seating and in 1961 leather upholstery was offered as an optional extra.

(130.97 sq cm) and the power went up from 46 bhp at 5,500 rpm to 56 bhp at 5,500 rpm.

The improvement in performance was welcome, for already small saloons, such as the Mini-Cooper, were almost capable of out-performing Spridgets. The 1,071-cc Mini-Cooper S, which admittedly cost £100 more, was about 8 mph faster and reached 50 mph 2 seconds sooner. It could carry four people and corner much faster and it was putting market pressure on the two-seater from within BMC itself. Moreover, the Triumph Spitfire appeared, with an 1,147-cc engine, which gave it a top speed of over 90 mph, and independent rear suspension. It was some time before enthusiasts realized that a well-located live axle was more satisfactory than an indifferent independent rear. The Spitfire nonetheless had an appealing specification, and a better ride, which could be discerned during a demonstration run. It also had wind-up windows and a more rounded sense of style.

The Spridget's 1,098-cc engine was not an unqualified success.

Ocelot-looking seat covers and the radio are optional extras on this Midget Mark I, but the seat belt anchorages were mandatory. The angle of this picture emphasizes the complete absence of rear-seat leg room. The angled tubes just behind the doors are to locate the hood irons.

account of the difference in basic price of a mere £27, which Purchase Tax magnified to £38 5s.

Less than a year-and-a-half after the dual model got under way, the Sprite 1100, as it was known, and the similarly improved Midget were announced. The change, for the Earls Court Motor Show, in October 1962, did not alter the model designations Sprite Mark II and Midget (never called the Mark I except retrospectively). The British Motor Corporation's revised A-Series engine was bored and stroked to bring the capacity to 1,098 cc, disc brakes were standardized, baulk-ring synchromesh and a clutch 1 in larger at 7¼ in diameter were installed and, compared with earlier models, the interior became quite luxurious.

The cylinder bores were increased from 62.94 mm (2.478 in) to 64.58 mm (2.543 in), while the longer-stroke crankshaft gave 83.72 mm (3.296 in) instead of 76.2 mm (3 in). Piston area increased from 19.29 sq in (124.46 sq cm) to 20.3 sq in

The MG 'family' on display in the grounds of Blenheim Palace in 1962. The strong styling then shared by the Spridgets and the MGB can be seen clearly in this picture, only the Big Healey — recently updated from the 100-Six model to become the 3000 — having a style of its own, with the accent on curved body lines.

An overhead shot of the Midget in its Mark II form, which indicates clearly the considerable space between the two seats caused by the transmission tunnel. The introduction of the Mark II brought a change to winding windows and, beneath the skin, half-elliptic rear springs.

Indicating how to fold a hood on a prototype Mark III Sprite, on which the door trim has yet to be fitted. The rear window should be folded in this way in order to protect the Vybak material. This is an interim hood, with the new windscreen attachments, but still with fully removable fabric.

Non-perforated disc wheels and exterior door handles identify this 1964 Mark II Midget. The central windscreen stay was an idea borrowed from the MGB.

It had a rather weak crankshaft, which made it feel rough at speed. On the credit side, the new model had Lockheed disc brakes, though the Healeys preferred Girlings developed straight from the original Dunlop patents. The Healeys' disc-brake conversions had been Girling, but BMC policy was to use Lockheed for cars with A-Series engines, and Girlings for cars with B-Series power units, so Lockheeds it had to be.

Amongst the difficulties of the disc-brake installation was that the front suspension and steering had been designed for drum-braked Austin A30 and Morris Minor, respectively, and limited the size of disc it was possible to use. With no servo, it was necessary to employ high-friction pads, which wore out rather quickly and would not stand high temperatures until lining materials improved. The pads were good enough for road use, but could be troublesome in competitions until friction materials arrived which were less likely to fade and would remain stable at high temperatures.

Carpet on the floor and on the space behind the seats and a padded roll along the bottom of the facia made the car a good deal more habitable.

This Mark II Midget, designated the GAN 3, was really the third variant of the model, the 'Mark 1½' having been known as the Midget 1100. The 1,098-cc engine developed 59 bhp at 5,750 rpm.

Two years later, the Sprite III/Midget II put the 1,098-cc engine right, with main bearings increased in diameter from 1⅞ in to 2 in, and the cylinder-head improved with better porting and larger inlet valves. Power output increased from 56 bhp to 59 bhp at 5,750 rpm, taking the top speed to over 90 mph and making the acceleration more of a match for the Spitfire. Neither car, however, was in the same league as the Mini-Cooper S.

Besides the engine, the 1964 Spridgets underwent a rather more fundamental change. The quarter-elliptic rear springs were at last abandoned in favour of half-elliptics, and the sidescreens were replaced by winding windows. Amongst the cosmetic touches was a redesigned facia, and a parcels shelf to replace the door pockets sacrificed to make room for the window mechanism.

The restricted bump and rebound of the rear wheels had always provided the Sprite with a lively ride. The accompanying stiffness at the rear contributed to the quick steering response, which may have suited sensitive drivers, but induced nervous tension in others. Commercially, it was probably wiser to make the car more bland, and ensure a wider appeal, even if this represented a lessening of its delightful precision.

Competition from the more softly sprung Spitfire lent urgency to the change, which also meant the springs having to absorb torque reaction instead of the radius arms. Removal of the arms had the advantage of reducing noise within the car, because the bush on the chassis cross-member behind the seats fed road noise and vibration straight into the structure. The half-elliptic arrangement also turned out to be no more expensive. Given the structural changes which had already taken place, it was only necessary to add mounting points for the springs and delete the torque arms. The five-leaf half-elliptics were cheaper than the 15-leaf quarter-elliptics.

Showroom appeal of the Mark III Sprite/Mark II Midget was considerably enhanced by the winding windows and revisions to the interior. The windows and swivelling quarter-lights meant a new windscreen, which in turn brought modifications to the hood. MG designed a new facia, with a black crackle finish and the speedometer and electronic tachometer angled towards the driver.

The loss of elbow room, because the doors were filled up with window winder, was a pity, but at least the car could now be

Abingdon's heyday. Sprites and Midgets crowd the production lines in the former leather works that Cecil Kimber transformed into one of the world's most famous sports car factories. Automation was never a strong suit, but industrial relations were a model of their kind.

The Austin-Healey Sprite Mark IV, which was outwardly identical to the Mark III, but was equipped with a detuned Mini-Cooper S engine of 1,275 cc developing 65 bhp at 6,000 rpm.

Disc front brakes became part of the standard specification of Sprites and Midgets in 1962, to the considerable relief of Spridget enthusiasts, who had found the earlier drum brakes to be marginal on performance.

locked. The hood was an interim affair, still detachable, but secured to the top rail of the windscreen with over-centre clips in preparation for the more substantial, convertible-style hood still under development by Les Ireland, Healey's body designer. The tension stay in the middle of the windscreen served the double purpose of providing a stable mounting for the rear-view mirror and supporting the windscreen top rail against the pull of the slipstream on the hood at high speed. MG had already used the ploy successfully on the MGB.

Ireland had been designing weather equipment for open cars since the days of the prewar Triumph Dolomite, and the full development of his new Sprite hood appeared at the introduction of the Mark IV and its companion Mark III Midget at the 1966 Earls Court Motor Show.

This used a detuned, 65-bhp version of the 1,275-cc Mini-Cooper S engine, giving it a further useful increase in performance against the Spitfire without any real sacrifice in economy. The A-Series engine was already 20 years old, but the Mini-Cooper had provided a great incentive for the development of increased power over the last five. It had been bored and

The MG Midget Mark III with the hood folded and tucked neatly behind a cover held down by Lift-the-Dot fasteners. The exterior door handles and locks had first appeared on the Mark II.

The improved hood of the Mark III, which is secured permanently to the rear of the cockpit instead of having to be detached and folded separately. Note also the larger window area provided.

stroked, reworked and rejigged, but the version chosen for the Spridget was new again, with a bore of 70.61 mm (2.78 in) and a stroke of 81.28 mm (3.2 in), the same as the Mini-Cooper S, but developing only 65 bhp at 6,000 rpm instead of 76 bhp. This enabled cheaper materials to be used, as it had smaller valves and a compression ratio of 8.8:1 instead of 9.7:1, achieved by dished piston crowns.

The 4.22:1 axle was continued at first, then replaced by the higher 3.9:1, which improved fuel consumption and made cruising less stressful on Britain's motorways, whose network, extending throughout the country, was producing an antipathy towards noisy cars with flapping hoods. Speed limits lay in the future, and already enthusiasts were looking less favourably on cars which could not be run more-or-less flat-out, in reasonable peace and quiet, on the new fast roads.

The new engine's crankshaft was soon modified as well. Pre-production cars used a standard material, which was changed to a nitrided crank in E40 steel for production cars, marked AEG 565. Nitriding proved too expensive, however, so a tuftrided version was used instead, with the same markings.

The ease with which the new convertible-style hood could be raised or lowered on Spridgets considerably widened the appeal of BMC's small sports cars in October 1966. Over-centre catches secured the hood to the windscreen rail and fasteners behind the door openings were undone if it was to be stowed away.

The Sprite in its Mark IV guise, with one or two fit problems around the right rear quarter of the hood. As on previous models, the Sprite lacked the chrome body strips which continued to adorn the Midget.

There was a proposal to use the full-blown 76-bhp Cooper S engine to meet the threatened competition from the Honda S800, reflecting the relative merits in Formula 3 and Formula 2 single-seater racing of the BMC A-Series and the Honda engines. But Honda began to look more towards saloon cars, and in any case, an additional 11 bhp would have given the Spridget a 100 mph-plus performance uncomfortably close to the 105-mph MGB.

Identifiable by the new 10-stud cylinder-head, the engine had long-skirt pistons with the normal two compression and one scraper ring, but to provide greater rubbing area and longer life, at the cost perhaps of some friction, the rings were wider than customary. The new hood was stowed under a neat cover, for which the cockpit opening was again enlarged slightly.

Following the introduction of the Mark IV Sprite and Mark III Midget, design and development work became the sole responsibility of MG. The manoeuvres that were to result in the formation of the British Leyland Motor Corporation were already under way. Alvis and Rover had joined forces in 1965 and the following year Jaguar-Daimler and BMC announced a link-up to be known as British Motor Holdings. Then Standard-Triumph-Leyland and Alvis-Rover joined together, and in 1968, the stage was set for the creation of a British Leyland conglomerate, which effectively brought together most of the native motor industry of Britain.

The Healeys' place in such a vast corporation was clearly anomalous. The employment of an outside consultancy to carry out product development work was anathema to the cost accountants, to whom it must have appeared a needless duplication of the work going on in the formal development departments of the firms which had been brought together. Surely, amongst such an assembly of skill and experience, there was *somebody* capable of doing the Healeys' work?

There probably was, but the Healeys had never been instructed to produce a car such as the Sprite. Instead, they had had the initiative and enterprise to turn up with the right design at the right time. As a result, a marque name had been created, which had acquired a style and prestige in the sports car world perhaps disproportionate to its worth in sheer engineering, or strict sales terms. Alas, its value was not visible to the new regime.

Rationalization often means merely finding the lowest common denominator, not the highest common factor. The design

By 1966 the Spridget's engine compartment was beginning to get quite crowded. Even on cars without the US Federal emission-control equipment, the closed-circuit breathing arrangements had become more complex, with the diaphragm seen to the right of the rocker cover oil filler cap.

The end of the road for Austin-Healey. From January 1971, the Sprite was to carry the prefix Austin, as the caption to this British Leyland publicity photograph indicated. However, this car still carries an Austin-Healey badge in the centre of the radiator grille.

The neat cover concealing the folded hood was a great improvement, but other 1966 modifications were less successful. The inside door handles had to be squeezed out of the way of the window-winding mechanism, and the hollows in the doors never made up for the lost elbow room, making the interior markedly less roomy. The black crackle facia and the angled instruments remained a feature of home-market cars to the end, and carpet had replaced the rubber floor covering.

mediocrity that was to play such an important rôle in the downfall of British Leyland and Lord Stokes replaced the innovatory spirit of the Healeys and their MG counterparts.

Projects of promise at Rover and MG, including a revised Mini and a Mini-based Midget, as well as the development programme of the big Healey, were stopped. Production of the 3000 ceased in December 1967.

The Sprite Mark IV, with the chassis prefix HAN 9, did not suffer such a clean-cut execution, but died from a thousand cuts instead.

The first stage was the withdrawal of the Mark IV HAN 9 from the United States and all other export markets in September 1969. Henceforward, only MG Midgets would go abroad. The Mark V Sprite HAN 10 was launched in October, along with the Midget GAN 5, but still called the Mark III, for the 1970 model year. The cars were 'Leylandized' with a common grille, a black oval and Leyland symbols as well as the MG and Austin-Healey

1971 marked the adoption of a commonized radiator grille for the Sprite and the Midget, with just a different badge in the middle. If enthusiasts for each make were disappointed, they might have been comforted had they known what was in store as regards front-end treatment in the years ahead.

badges. Cast wheels, black sills and seat trim which featured narrow centre panels with horizontal ribbing were included in the package of cosmetics. For a time, the windscreen surround was black as well, but withdrawal from the United States meant it was no longer necessary to meet this supposed quirk of federal regulations, so it reverted to matt silver.

In October 1970, for the 1971 model year, the Mark V/Mark III was given an improved heater, an interior courtesy lamp, a luggage boot lamp, and Rostyle instead of cast wheels. The fuel tank was enlarged from 6 Imperial gallons (27.27 litres, 7.2 US

The cockpit of a 1971 Sprite featuring more behind-the-knees bolstering in the seat cushions. Even the instrument markings were identical to those on the Midget.

gallons) to 7 (31.82, 8.4), and the rear wheelarches rounded, instead of being squared-off. Only UK Austin dealers now sold the car, and further marketing changes were on the way, because the licence to use the Healey name ran out on December 31, 1970. British Leyland, having taken up the old BMC contract with the Healeys, were, however, allowed to sell Austin-Healeys until June 1971, in order for stock to be run out, or a new contract negotiated. No renewal was proposed.

Henceforward, the car would be known as an Austin Sprite. Then, in February 1971, the decision was taken to end even that by the summer shutdown in July. All that remained was to change Austin dealers' franchise arrangements, enabling them to sell MG Midgets, and the life of the Sprite was snuffed out. When the Healey name was dropped in 1970, chassis prefixes became AAN, the tally of Austin Sprites, all sold in the United Kingdom, coming to 1,022 out of the grand total of 129,532.

In 1972, radial-ply tyres were standardized for the Midget III,

Only the badges on the facia and the steering wheel boss identify this Midget from a Sprite. The doors are now fully trimmed, with padded sills, and have substantial pulls.

1971 was a time when individual marque names were being de-emphasized and cars were increasingly being adorned by the British Leyland 'catherine wheel' corporate symbol, to the dismay of many.

the dynamo was replaced by an alternator and the front suspension was raised by half-an-inch. The following year, there were more detail changes including hazard warning lights and an anti-roll bar at the front, and the tonneau cover became standard equipment.

Time was running out, however, for the venerable 1,275-cc engine. Legislation pending in the United States implied unacceptable power and cost penalties. Safety regulations meant weighty front and rear bumpers. With seven or eight out of every 10 Spridgets going to the United States, meeting US regulations was vital, although European ECE 15 emission regulations had soon to be satisfied as well. By 1974, further changes were inevitable.

The most fundamental was the adoption of the engine from the car's old rival, the Triumph Spitfire. The 1,491-cc four-cylinder power unit proved to be about the same size, and the only modification needed to make it fit was a redesign of the exhaust manifold and new air filters.

Like the engine it replaced, the Triumph could trace its ancestry to a rather less distinguished unit from a small family saloon. Like the old Morris Minor/Austin A35 engine, it also began at 803 cc, fitted to the 1953 Standard 8. As developed for the Spitfire, it produced 65 bhp, at 500 rpm less than the 65 bhp of the old 1,275-cc Cooper S. Torque showed a useful increase, from 72 lb ft to 76.5 lb ft (9.957 mkg to 10.579 mkg) at the same 3,000 rpm, and the gearing remained the same, with the 3.9:1 final drive and the 145—12-inch tyres giving 16.4 mph per 1,000 rpm.

For the first time since the introduction of baulk-ring synchromesh in 1962, there was a major change to the gearbox.

Radial-ply Pirelli Cinturatos were amongst the standard tyres being fitted to the two-piece Spridget wheels by 1971. Long after the original one-piece lift-up front body section had disappeared, the 'join' line remained a Spridget feature.

The commonized radiator grille, this time badged as an MG, and accompanied by a black-framed windscreen and squared-off rear wheelarches, identify this as a 1970 Midget.

Other identification features of the 1970 model year included reversing lights, a transverse tailpipe silencer and split rear bumpers.

This was a new all-synchromesh unit based on the single-rail design evolved for the 1.3 Morris Marina, with wider ratios than before, and it came with a new propeller shaft.

The extra torque was not only welcome, but necessary. The car's weight had gone up by a further 200 lb, the bulk of it due to the '5 mph' bumpers, making the kerb weight of around 1,850 lb (839 kg) a far cry from the 1,400 lb (635 kg) of the Mark I Sprite. The bumpers were moulded in urethane foam over a steel armature base, with the body structure suitably reinforced to deal with the loads. A further consequence of the changes, which followed rear-end impact testing, was the reversion to the old squared-off rear wheelarch, providing extra metal to resist body distortion in accidents coming from behind.

The ride height was raised by a further inch, by a change to the front cross-member mounting and recambering the rear springs, to meet the bumper-height requirements, but it altered the handling for all time. The extra weight may have helped the ride through the inertia effects at the car's extremities, but the changes to the suspension brought more body roll, and made it altogether less lively, despite the improved performance. Overall length

By 1974, the Sprite had gone, as had the 'lightening' holes in the steering wheel spokes, and the switchgear had changed to the rocker type for safety reasons. Safety considerations also decreed the head restraints, and the doors had sprouted enormous noise-inducing mirrors. There was an interior light, and the radio was optional.

A round-wheelarched car from 1971-2. However, the squared-off shape was to return later in order to stiffen the resistance to rear-end collision damage. In the opinion of many, the removal of the chrome body strips from the sides of later Midgets had enhanced the car's lines.

Introduced in October 1974, the new soft nose for the Midget was the most noticeable feature of a drastically changed car. The most fundamental changes in the history of the Spridget included the use of the Triumph Spitfire engine and Morris Marina gearbox, and revised suspension settings which altered the car's handling for all time.

some overheating problems amongst early soft-nosed Midgets, and the cooling system had to be changed to take account of it. Detail alterations were made in 1976 and 1977 in view of the ever-tighter emission laws, and the rear axle ratio was changed to 3.72:1 in September 1977.

The 1,493-cc Spitfire engine transformed the under-bonnet scene in the Midget. Amongst the improvements was a sealed cooling system, but the battery was as difficult to top up as ever, and there was only a marginal increase in power and torque over the former 1,275-cc BMC engine.

increased by just over 3½ in (8.9 cm). Hazard warning lights, an anti-roll bar and the tonneau cover and rail were standardized.

Merely meeting legislative changes began to absorb so much time and effort at development departments, not only at MG but throughout the industry, that routine annual model facelifts became a thing of the past. The not undesirable abandonment of planned obsolescence was achieved for the wrong reasons. What this meant in the case of the Midget was that no major revisions took place from 1974 onwards. Those which did were relatively minor, in the interests of rationality, necessity, or both.

In January 1977, head restraints were included in the standard specification, and in April, inertia-reel safety belts were included. A year later, the radio console was added, along with two-speed wipers and a brake-failure warning light.

The small air intake within the urethane bumpers resulted in

The soft-nose treatment was not confined to the Midget. Here is an MG line-up in 1978, towards the end of the marque's illustrious career as an Abingdon-built sports car, comprising an MGB, an MGB GT and a Midget and revealing a strong family appearance.

At the same time, the instruments on left-hand-drive cars were 'commonized' with those on the MGB, and those on right-hand-drive cars with the Spitfire. Although now withdrawn even from Europe, the Midget conformed with EEC Type Approval, with door mirrors, and a three-part exhaust system with a silencer across the rear of the car. In October 1978, a dual-line braking system was added.

All that was left of the original Sprite was the floor pan, visible in the upsweep of the sill behind the front wheelarch (a relic of the Mark I's opening front), and the front suspension and steering. The car had put on weight, losing most, although not all of its sprightliness.

Only the fun remained until, at the end of 1979, the last Midget was made. The entire future of the Abingdon factory was in the balance, the whole destiny of MG under threat.

The protests evoked reflected the reservoir of goodwill which the MG car had accumulated since Cecil Kimber created the marque in the early-1920s, and which had been shared with the Sprite since the production and development of the smallest Austin-Healey moved to Abingdon in the late-1950s.

In June 1976 the United States market was offered the MG Midget Special, with AM/FM radio, chrome-finished luggage rack, wheel trim rings and a distinctive side stripe in an attempt to make up for indifferent handling and a lacklustre performance.

CHAPTER 4

Spridgets on the road

The performance appeal of a low-cost sports car

The technological climate in which the Spridget ended its days was very different from the balmy sports car summer in which it was born. In 1958, open cars were still in vogue, still representing the characteristic sports-racing car. It was thought rather dashing to drive with the top down, and closed cars, or 'fug boxes', were dismissed as effete. The more resistant one was to saloons the better, and it was a matter of some pride to leave the top stowed away in all but the very depths of winter.

Le Mans was much more of a sports car Mecca than it was destined to become; the Ferraris, Porsches and Aston Martins that raced there were mostly open. The mid-engined revolution lay in the future, and aerodynamics was a matter of frontal area and streamlining, rather than wings and spoilers. The ground-effect car was no more than an academic theory, and although closed cars were recognized as more efficient, the open-car tradition was so firmly rooted that sports cars were still not expected to have a roof.

As a performer, the Sprite was demonstrably middling. Contemporary cars which reached 100 mph were exceptional and generally expensive; those which did 90 mph were unusual. The average maximum speed of 40 cars road tested by *The Motor* between February 1957 and August 1958 was 81.42 mph. They included the Sprite, following its launch in May 1958, when it recorded 82.8 mph. It reached 50 mph in 13.7 sec; the class average was 13.98 sec. So, bearing in mind the substantial numbers of older cars still on the road, many dating from the 1930s, it was clearly able to keep ahead of most of the traffic.

But amongst the better contemporary sports cars, it fared less well. The AC Ace-Bristol, for example, and the six-cylinder Austin-Healey were 115-mph cars, the AC reaching 50 mph in 7 sec, the big Healey in 8.5 sec. But the AC was a hand-built £2,095 car, and the BT 7 Healey cost £1,175 without even overdrive and hardtop, compared with the Sprite's 1959 price of £631.

More strictly comparable was the MGA. At a price of £940 it did 96 mph, and reached 50 mph in 9.1 sec. The Triumph TR3 cost just over the £1,000 mark, reached 109 mph, and did 50 mph in 8.9 sec.

The Sprite's only rivals at the price were the Berkeley and the Lotus Seven. Only the Lotus could reach 50 mph faster, neither was as quick on the straight in standard form, and neither could compete in finish, strength, or comfort.

In economy, only the 62-mph Berkeley, with 47 mpg, could approach the Sprite's 43 mpg. There was no comparative 'urban cycle' routine, but *The Motor's* testers covered 1,696 miles on 50.5 gallons, giving 33.6 mpg (8.4 litres per 100 km). The constant-speed figures were:
52.5 mpg (5.38 litres per 100 km) at 30 mph (48.28 kph)
54.5 mpg (5.18 litres per 100 km) at 40 mph (64.37 kph)
53.5 mpg (5.28 litres per 100 km) at 50 mph (80.47 kph)
38.0 mpg (7.43 litres per 100 km) at 60 mph (96.56 kph)
36.0 mpg (7.85 litres per 100 km) at 70 mph (112.65 kph)
Acceleration times were:
0-30 mph 5.1 sec.
0-40 mph 8.5 sec.
0-50 mph 13.7 sec.
0-60 mph 20.5 sec.
0-70 mph 31.1 sec.
Standing ¼-mile 21.8 sec.

The original 'frog-eye' Sprite represented a new concept in low-cost sports cars on its announcement in 1958, its basic simplicity of design contributing not only to a relatively low purchase price, but also to attractively low maintenance costs. Its driver appeal, however, was vested in its taut, nimble handling, with finger-tip steering response, characteristics which were to make it a popular choice as a club competition car.

Weight distribution was 55/45 front/rear, and the car recorded maximum speeds in the gears of 25 mph, 39 mph and 65 mph.

The Sprite weighed around 195 lb (88 kg) less than the A35, and a more substantial 390 lb (177 kg) less than the Morris Minor 1000. With 10 to 12 in (25 to 30 cm) less in height and proportionately reduced frontal area the performance was 10 mph livelier than either at roughly similar cost, and with pretty much the same state of tune.

The yardstick against which the Sprite's appeal was measured thus fell between the contemporary sports cars and the contemporary small saloons. At saloon car prices, it was able to offer more performance, even though it had no pretensions about competing in the high-speed league. The Mini and its derivatives, together with the new standards which they set, lay in the future; the Continental industry had nothing like it, and the Rising Sun had not yet appeared over the Far East horizon.

It was hardly surprising, therefore, to find the car welcomed by the press and public alike, sales reaching an encouraging 8,729

Few road cars have been so accessible for maintenance. Lifting the front revealed not only the engine and ancillaries, but the front suspension, steering and brakes as well. The supporting rod gave additional insurance against failure of the back struts which, were they to give way, would have given a new meaning to the term 'alligator bonnet' to hapless mechanics.

between May and December 1958, and 21,566 in the whole of 1959. Donald Healey's intuition about the sports car market had proved right. He had identified the requirement, supplied the car to fit it and was about to profit from his good judgment and skill.

The 8.3:1 compression allowed the Sprite to use the middle of the three fuel grades generally available in Britain, but the 9.0:1 option was there for those prepared (and many were) to use the 100-octane premium petrol coming on to the market. The rationing that followed the Suez crisis in 1956 had ended 12 months before the launch of the Sprite, but the cost of a gallon had climbed from its comfortable 4s 6d (22½p) to 4s 8d (23.3p), and seemed likely to break the 5s (25p) barrier before long in what

was known as the Inner Distribution Zone.

The 5,000 rpm employed as a matter of course, with cautionary markings as high as 5,500 rpm and 6,000 rpm, represented a fairly free-revving engine for 1958. Keen drivers, however, found the gap between second and third gears too wide, a criticism acknowledged in the development of a close-ratio box by BMC, which was offered as an option on the Mark I, and later became standard equipment on the Mark II car. New Mark I gear-changes were sometimes prone to stiffness when the gearbox oil became hot, on account of production tolerances closing-up, but like the rest of the car, the gearboxes were, on the whole, fairly reliable.

The trunking on the left carried the fresh air to the heater, but unfortunately its intake was close to exhaust height and noxious fumes could fill a Sprite in traffic. Crude inner mudguards were effective in keeping the engine clean, but the low-mounted intake could ship flood water. Holes in each chassis member projecting from beneath the radiator served to locate the bonnet.

Mark I handling was a matter of wrist movement rather than conscious steering; deftness was essential, and heavy-handed drivers, as a rule, disliked it. Road-testers of early cars complained about a tendency to pull to the right during acceleration, and to the left on the over-run, an engineer's explanation of the effects of torque reaction, which could lead him to imagine a trace of rear-wheel steering. Body roll was negligible, but the standard 5.20—13 tyres, generally Dunlop Gold Seal, would squeal as the front wheels imposed their modest understeer. Yet the balance of the car was very satisfactory. Drivers over 5 ft 10 in tall sat too close to the steering wheel to enjoy the long-arm posture made fashionable by aces such as Stirling Moss and Jack Brabham, in those days still visible in the cockpits of Grand Prix cars. The upswept part of the chassis platform, carrying all the stresses of the rear suspension, was so close to the back of the seat that even at full rearward adjustment many drivers found the elbow room within the hollow doors indispensable.

Drawbacks of the Mark I included the brakes, which really were only adequate for touring. Three or four stops from 60 mph would produce the familiar smell of hot linings, and a fifth or sixth would send the pedal to the floor. Competition drivers found it necessary to fit the Warwick disc-brake conversion, together with wire wheels to create more ventilation round the brakes than was possible with the standard perforated disc

The battery was the rearmost occupant of the engine compartment. Inspection of the electrolyte level, consequently, was never easy and filling was problematical. As a result, Mark Is often suffer from corrosion in this area.

Morris rack-and-pinion steering and Austin front suspension contributed to the sensitive handling of the Sprite, but the modest size of the drum brakes was a less satisfactory feature.

wheels. Until the advent of the Mini, Sprite wheels were amongst the smallest into which brakes were being squeezed; heavy demands within such a small compass were unusual, and development had yet to catch up.

Once a Sprite's shock absorbers became weak, the front suspension would reach the bump stops, and the forward part of the front sub-frame would all too easily grind itself away on the crown of single-track roads. The low intake was susceptible to shipping water straight into the engine compartment. The interior wings trapped most of the road spray, but taking what sailors call 'green water' over the bows would quickly drown a Mark I.

Rally enthusiasts were critical of the absence of a fly-off handbrake, particularly in view of the sea-front driving tests which were such a feature of rallies at the time. The Sprite's manoeuvrability, the good visibility, and the 2¼-turns lock-to-lock steering made it ideal for this sort of competition, which

neither went far nor fast enough to show up the deficiencies of the brakes.

While the Mark I had perhaps more than its share of the qualities that were to make it one of Britain's best-loved small sports cars, luxurious it was not. The door handles could only be reached when the hood was up by unbuttoning a corner of the celluloid sidescreen.

Hand signalling was still recommended by driving instructors, and the tiny gap was supposed to allow an arm out for the purpose. Not for Sprite owners the clever little telescopic strut on the sprung flap, which allowed MGA drivers to wag an arm in comfort.

The Mark I's standard sidescreens were seldom photographed on road-test cars, and never in publicity pictures. In time, they scratched and became opaque, making the more expensive sliding ones *de rigeur*. The wrap-round window in the hood, on the other

The rear-suspension layout of an early Sprite, with the torque-reaction arm located above the 15-leaf quarter-elliptic spring and part of the lever-arm shock absorber just visible inboard of them. The body mountings for the springs and arms became rust points on earlier cars.

The rear suspension viewed from the inboard side, showing the mounting of the quarter-elliptic spring on a bracket welded to the axle casing and the location of the Armstrong shock absorber between chassis plate and axle bracket. The torque-reaction arm can be seen behind the elbow of the shock absorber link.

hand, only clouded over after years, provided the Vybak material was properly looked after, and the hood folded according to the book when it was stowed.

The change from stud-fixing to the slot in the top screen rail was essential. As *The Motor* put it: 'Unluckily, the pattern of air flow around the body at speeds above 60 mph tends to flutter the hood, and blows rainwater or insects into the body through gaps which open up between the easy-to-erect hood and the top of the windscreen, and between the windscreen and the sidescreens.'

Unlucky indeed. Yet the removable hood was a triumph of simplicity, and with the heater supplying a sufficiently generous current of air to create a positive pressure within, the hood-up Mark I was astonishingly draught-proof and snug. The heater was sufficiently powerful to make open motoring not merely possible, but quite pleasurable in cold weather with the passenger's seat covered with the tonneau, the sidescreens up and the fan belting out a stream of warm air round the driver.

Regulation of the water flow through the heater matrix meant an expedition under the bonnet to the cylinder-block water tap, but this was a rare chore, usually carried out seasonally. There were so many places for air to escape from the cockpit of a Mark I Sprite that, except in unusually hot weather, a stream of warmth through the central vents or — if the spring-loaded doors were shut — up the demister slots hardly mattered.

The absence of a lock and key for the luggage compartment turned out to be of little concern to most owners, even though BMC's earnest marketing men considered it a tangible sales disincentive. Small items could remain in the rearmost extremity

The author's first Mark I Sprite in 1959. Badge bar, additional lamps and mirrors and non-standard headlights are the trappings of a Sprite enthusiast.

of the boot, safe from retrieval even by their owners. To gain access, the seat backs were folded, and looking for anything near the number-plate end swallowed a searcher at least to his middle, which action also blocked out most of the available light. Burglars had to know where to look, and be prepared to be agile if they wanted to steal anything in a hurry.

The spare wheel was fixed to the floor of the boot with webbing looped round three cleats, and there was a loose plastic boot liner which achieved little beyond transferring dirt from the spare wheel to the luggage. Punctures in wet weather, particularly with suitcases aboard, were messy and fractious affairs.

It was hardly surprising, therefore, that amongst the earliest Sprite accessories was a luggage grid for mounting outside the tail, and an external wheel fixing. Care had to be taken not to overload these, however, because the large panel which made up the rear deck was liable to buckle, leaving a crease which was

The quick steering response of Sprites and Midgets made them formidable competitors in driving tests. The pronounced tuck-in of the offside front wheel is evidence of how hard this competitor on an RAC Championship event in 1964 is trying.

almost impossible to eradicate. People were not allowed to sit on the tail of a Mark I for the same reason.

There was no denying that the Sprite had few frills, yet the exposure of the structural gussets within the tail, or the plainness of the folded-over metalwork under the bonnet, somehow lent an air of those same sports-racing cars that so captured the imagination at Le Mans. Cars stripped to their essentials were somehow more businesslike than those weighed down with chrome, or heavy with carpets. Enthusiasts interpreted the spartan nature as evidence of being built down to a weight rather than down to a price. Ferraris often had bare floors with structural members showing through, and a non-cancelling flasher switch simply did not matter.

What did matter was the precision of the gear-change, the delightful lightness of the steering, and the way the car could be hustled along winding roads with all the air, and much of the

excitement, of doing twice the speed. For enthusiasts learning the virtues of a well-balanced sporting car it was ideal. For old hands who had forgotten what one was like it was a pleasure.

On the introduction of the MG Midget, in July 1961, there was not much the motoring press could do except repeat what they had said about the Mark II Sprite in June. It is worth noting, in these inflationary times, that the Mark II actually cost less than the Mark I had three years before, and not only through changes in the rate of Purchase Tax. The basic price was £3 lower, despite the changes, the extra power, and the addition in weight of around ½ cwt (25 kg).

Yet, was the facelift necessary? Had BMC persevered with an even cheaper, mechanically improved Sprite, might the sales decline still have been arrested? As things turned out, it was barely stemmed.

However, the near-identical twins were well-received, even

How times have changed. This BMC publicity photograph, featuring an early Midget, seems to imply that it was an ideal car for taking the girl friend out to the country pub for a quick pint. In those carefree days there was little sensitivity to the perils of associating drinking and driving.

taking account of the enhanced expectations of the customers. Nevertheless, noise would become a source of irritation as other cars grew quieter — especially closed cars — and speeds tended to rise. The small doors drew criticism, their size restricted by the requirements of strength in the vital area around the scuttle.

The conventional front-opening bonnet restricted access to the engine, with the distributor and the fuel pump low down on opposite sides; masked by the carburettors, the dynamo and the heater trunking, they had suddenly become very difficult to reach. The chassis needed greasing at 12 points, eight of them round the front wheels, now within non-opening wings. Maintenance had been easy when the bonnet lifted to reveal all, but was more likely to be postponed, or overlooked altogether, now that the grease points were all out of sight.

The new lockable luggage space was welcome, together with the other general enhancements, yet there was little corresponding improvement in comfort. Nor was there much increase in performance. Indeed, the new car was slightly slower, with a blunter approach to aerodynamics, especially in the critical region around the new headlamps. The old shape had better

penetration, so top speed now suffered. Better breathing at high rpm, and some testing with the hardtop in place to improve streamlining, brought about improvements at the upper end of the acceleration range, but up to 40 mph the extra weight told, and the new car was slower off the mark. Top-gear performance was better as a result of the hefty increase in torque, and the fuel consumption was also marginally improved.

The car only came alive, however, when it was equipped with an 1,100-cc engine at the 1962 London Motor Show. Top speed went up to almost 90 mph, and the standing quarter-mile edged a little closer to the magic 20 sec, putting it on a par with the exotic Alfa Romeo Giulietta ti and the racy Riley 1.5. However, it was still not *that* swift, and it was possible to out-drag a Sprite with a determined Vanden Plas Princess 3-litre automatic.

No less than 20 sec was chopped off the 0-80 mph time, changing up on the new electronic tachometer (the troublesome gearbox on the back of the dynamo had at last been done away

with) at a modest 5,000 rpm. The amber warning between 5,500 rpm and 6,000 rpm, with a red between 6,000 rpm and 7,000 rpm, although *A* assured its readers that valve bounce limited 6,300 rpm.

Noise continued to draw criticism, with conv as virtually impossible owing to the racket fr that, in turn, was drowned by the roar of t ring synchromesh proved a useful aid to r changes, and tyre technology caught up w in the form of Dunlop C 41 tyres, still kn They helped the new disc brakes reco pedal pressure, and for all time performance of every car.

At first glance a formidable array of luggage to be accommodated in the rear compartment of a Midget, but slim-line cases help the illusion of impressive boot capacity.

Enthusiasm
for safety's sa
The new e
transverse-engi
Mini concept a
sprung MG 11
engine was alm
periods of vibrat
which persisted u
years later. The g
Motor's complaint
fumes from other t
alongside the passe
The ride and han
bears examination.
rubber bump stops

Nearly
in fact n
least some o

A wire-wheeled Mark II Midget, with wind-down windows, hinged quarter-lights and exterior door handles, kicking up the dust as its ability to make a tight turn on a loose surface is demonstrated.

for restoring Sprites to original specification ought, e, to stop short of 'period' tyres.

gine was derived from that of the ADO 16, the ned range of saloons which scaled-up the Issigonis nd introduced, amongst others, the Hydrolastic-0. The top half of the wider-bore, longer-stroke st the same as in the MG, but it suffered from on which set the gear-lever sizzling, a problem ntil the Sprite III/Midget II modifications two wing fussiness of road-testers was reflected in about the low air intake drawing in exhaust affic, and the way the handbrake disappeared er seat in the 'off' position.

ing of the last quarter-elliptic-sprung Sprite imited travel of the rear axle led to the becoming a more integral part of the

springing media than was either customary or probably desirable. Yet the integrity of the structure was such that Sprites and Midgets usually remained rattle-free and unfatigued. Sports cars were still expected to feel firm, well-damped and taut. The E-Type Jaguar was only just setting new standards of roadworthiness and comfort, and it would be some time before demands for a supple ride would reach the level of the Spridget.

So far as roadholding was concerned, it was accepted that what was still conventional, namely a front engine and rear-wheel drive, was no longer a match for small front-drive cars such as the Mini-Cooper. The mid-engined concept was still remote, and generally thought of as impractical for road cars. Thus, sports cars were still expected to behave much as they had in the 1950s; their rivals may have caught up, but they had not yet overtaken.

The Sprite's body roll was negligible, and quickly checked on entering a corner, yet it was accompanied by a discernible side-

The Spridget support industry offered proprietary four-way flashing hazard warning lights some 10 years before the factory got round to fitting them. The wheel-changer seems to be taking no chances, however. The price, at the time, from Britax was a modest £1.12.6 (£1.62½).

float on the quarter-elliptic springs and flexible bushes of the rear suspension. Heavy-handedness could result in this developing into a lurch, or a swerve, sometimes misinterpreted as rear-axle steer. Once set up for a corner, however, the car would stabilize along the line until the rear wheels progressively broke their grip of the road. The moment of breakaway could be postponed by increasing the rear tyre pressures, but the warning time would be proportionately diminished.

Bumpy corners could catch the rear axle on the hop, particularly if they were encountered at light sideways g, when the springs' lateral loadings would permit larger vertical deflections, bouncing the axle against the stops. Consequently, the harder the car was cornered, the more it seemed to like it because it became less bump-sensitive as heavy lateral loadings made the springs tighten-up. This valuable characteristic was useful to the hard-driving competitors rallying on rough, unmade surfaces in the farthest-flung regions of the Continent.

The softer upholstery of the 1100 Sprite and Midget emphasized the cars' unsuitability for drivers over about 5 ft 10 in tall. Lack of rearward seat adjustment meant that long-legged drivers found their knees jammed against the wheel. Against this, carpets and the padded roll on the facia brought a sophisticated look which the earlier cars had lacked.

So, the fundamental change in character began. It carried on with the smoother, wide-bearing engine of 1964, but the changes for the Mark III Sprite/Mark II Midget were farther-reaching than that. Winding windows, a new facia and the change-over to half-elliptic springs at the rear came with a car now capable of a top speed of nearly 95 mph (153 kph). Acceleration was improved, with the standing quarter-mile now under the 20-seconds mark, and 0-80 mph within striking distance of half-a-minute. Fuel consumption hardly suffered at all, even though weight continued its inexorable climb, while the car was now a match through the gears for the recently-superseded MGA.

The new rear springs conferred some advantage in reducing unsprung weight by dispensing with the torque arms and mounting brackets, thereby allowing more travel at a softer rate. The most obvious change was the absence of the famous lurch and the banishment of the rear-wheel steering effect, which had been more apparent than real in any case.

Instead, the car was now blander and less likely to catch out the clumsy. It could no longer be accused of twitchiness, indeed many Sprite enthusiasts saw the change as evidence of soggy degeneracy and decline. The back axle hopped more, although rear-end breakaway remained progressive enough. The car had neutral steering characteristics, so that in the wet the driver could control front or rear breakaway more or less as he chose. Fortunately, nobody saw fit to build-in the steering sogginess that might have been a natural corollary of the softening-up of the rear.

The ride was certainly improved, and from that point of view the changes were opportune because the Spitfire was now firmly established on the market, and rivalry between the makes had become keen. The Triumph was roomier and rather less stolid-looking, but although the ride was smoother, the tuck-in of the rear wheels under the influence of the swing-axle suspension thoroughly spoiled the handling.

The Sprite now covered pavé without bringing the bump stops quite so much into play, and the sturdy frame could withstand ill-treatment without the destructive scuttle shake under which some open cars would literally come apart at the seams. The winding windows filled up what had hitherto been elbow room, and together with the new windscreen, this improved visibility greatly when the hood was up. The hood fabric still had to be stowed in the boot, taken out, and thrown over the hood sticks when it rained, but it was attached by a couple of over-centre clips, which held it down to the top rail of the screen. This was probably a better means of fixing, in view of the higher speeds of which the new car was capable, but rather less easy to carry out.

The flimsy shelf underneath the facia was supposed to replace the roomy door pockets, and the re-arrangement of the instruments turned out to be practical, if no more elegant. The door locks lost a certain amount of their credibility because the inside latches remained so easily reached by unbuttoning a corner of the hood. Conversely, the handles were wretchedly difficult to get at from the inside. Self-parking screen wipers and manual screen washers were standard, but a headlamp flasher cost extra.

The Midget III/Sprite IV of 1966 turned out to be faster still. Eight years' development saw the top speed edge closer to 100 mph, although the car's persistent weight problem (it had gone up by around 2 cwt) meant that it failed to show the customary improvement in acceleration. The diaphragm-spring clutch was smoother, but gearboxes on this and subsequent models all appeared noisier than those on earlier cars, particularly in the indirect gears.

Thicker seat backs further reduced the amount of driver leg-room, and nobody over about 5 ft 8 in tall could now sit anywhere but unnaturally close to the wheel. The new hood attached to the rear deck could be raised and lowered from inside the car by someone with a tolerably long reach, at the expense of needing a bit more muscle than before.

The performance still needed fairly free use of the gearbox, with the revs kept above about 4,000 rpm to obtain really brisk cross-country speeds. Fortunately, the free-revving nature of the engine helped, and it was so smooth that several road-testers, finding it easy to over-rev, advised a keen watch on the danger markings on the tachometer, and suggested gear-changes at not more than 6,300 rpm.

Noise, however, remained a problem. Spridgets never had any sound damping, and except perhaps in some hard-topped versions, it would probably have made little difference anyway. Engine noise and wind noise continued to drown out the radio, perhaps saying more for the expectations of drivers in the mid-1960s than it does about the traditional small, sports two-seaters from which the car sprang.

Over-cooling was sometimes a problem with the Mark III, as with most Spridgets except the Mark I and the early versions of the squashy-bumpered cars. *Autocar* commented that they never managed to get their test car above about 162°F (72°C), which was just about the thermostat-opening point.

The extra weight led to higher fuel consumption during acceleration, leading in turn to demands for enlargement of the six-gallon fuel tank. At an overall 28-29 mpg, this meant looking for petrol stations at intervals of 150 miles, a nuisance for touring in daytime, and downright exasperating after dark, when pumps could be few and far between.

By the time of the 1969 facelift, the Spridget and Spitfire stood almost alone in the world. There was hardly any other small, open two-seater in quantity production anywhere, and none that bore comparison in terms of performance, economy and price. The engine was still in a milder state of tune than the MG version of the Austin-Morris 1100 saloon, which was permitted an

The Mark III version of the Sprite, with 1,098-cc engine developing 59 bhp at 5,750 rpm and half-elliptic rear springs in place of the earlier quarter-elliptics. The wire wheels, which were optional, are fitted here with Dunlop's high-hysteresis C41 tyres, which thoroughly transformed wet-road grip.

additional 5 bhp (making it a trace faster in some respects), but in an effort to meet the problem of under-gearing the axle ratio was changed in 1970 from 4.22:1 to 3.9:1. The mph per 1,000 rpm in top gear went up from 15.37 to 16.44, and radial-ply tyres such as the Michelin ZX were now a frequently-fitted option. These marginally altered the mph-per-1,000 rpm figure.

Top speed went up a fraction, but instead of being achieved at 6,000 rpm, the peak of the power curve, it came in at around 5,700 rpm. Acceleration was affected, but by a barely measurable amount, and the new ratio probably improved fuel consumption, but once again by such a small fraction as to be scarcely significant. A welcome change for this model was the inclusion of self-propping stays for the bonnet and boot-lid.

In January 1972, the rounded rear wheelarch came in for its brief reign, and the wheels were the proper Rostyle design, not the imitative type employed previously. Fuel-tank capacity went up to a useful seven gallons, and other alterations included better carpets, a larger gear-lever knob and changes to the door handles and switchgear.

The Sprite, of course, was gone by this time, and all the cars coming from Abingdon were MG Midgets. Soon, the requirements of the American market would change the car almost out of recognition, making the 1972-4 Midget arguably one of the most attractive propositions for collectors. It had acquired most of the technical developments and creature comforts it would ever have, and the looks and handling were probably at their best since the frog-eyed car had been dropped. Moreover, as the final Mark before the rubber-bumpered cars, Midgets of this vintage remain the best-preserved of all the unadulterated versions.

Testers and owners alike found that all the Marks up to 1974 shared common vices and virtues. Transmissions came in for criticism on account of noise and the absence of synchromesh on first — a shortcoming which became steadily more noticeable as ever more mundane and ordinary saloons were so equipped. The gears, especially first, were generally noisy by comparison with the increasingly refined production boxes coming out of factories with the latest automated, electronically-controlled gear-cutting machinery. Enthusiasts were supposed to be more interested in fast gear-changes than whine in the indirects, and the Midget's change was always a model of what a sports car should be, but comparisons with run-of-the-mill cars were inevitable.

The brakes remained efficient. The disc-and-drum arrangement was never given any servo assistance, but with such a light car, with a comparatively modest performance, they were always working well within their capacity. Whereas the Spitfire could be equipped with overdrive, which refined it at high speeds, the Midget remained noisy at speed, once again a characteristic which became more marked with the passing years and the general improvement of contemporary small family cars. Handling also continued to look less acceptable by comparison. Although drivers brought up on rear-drive, so-called conventional cars found the balance and feel of the car a delight, and the responsive steering all that the sports car enthusiast could desire, understeer gradually became more pronounced. Axle tramp on rough roads had been banished from other cars, along with drive-line vibrations and a choppy ride. Yet the Midget still caught the imagination with its torsionally stiff structure, its good visibility with the top down (except for the rather messy area round the quarter-lights) and its total absence of vice.

Two arch-rivals' cornering behaviour was evaluated by *Autocar* during a comparative test session on the MIRA road course near Nuneaton. Here, the Midget demonstrates mild understeer and moderate body roll.

The Triumph Spitfire, on the other hand, gets thoroughly out of shape, with the rear wheel tucking under — a penalty of the swing-axle arrangement — and the car in consequence displaying an uncomfortable degree of oversteer.

The Arkley sports car, seen here on the left in the company of a Mark IV Midget, is a Spridget conversion recalling the idiom of the Mark I Sprite, but with different front and rear treatment and featuring wind-down windows and a later-model hood.

'Controversial' was the euphemism most often applied to the styling changes of 1974. To most people the safety *appliqué* was, and remains, ugly. The good proportions of the car were destroyed, and so was the balance and feel which had given so much fun to so many drivers.

The new car was not all bad, however. To make up for around 200 lb (90.7 kg) increase in weight, the Spitfire engine brought a welcome increase in power and torque. But the ride height was increased by an inch to meet the regulation bumper height required for colliding with larger automobiles in North America. The North Americans have since very sensibly changed to smaller cars, also designed to the same daft set of rules, which only goes to show how boxed-in one can get through having cars designed by bureaucrats.

The change reduced the roll stiffness, and instead of the precise, neutral characteristics which the Spridget had enjoyed from its inception, the car now oversteered. It had been effected despite the heavier engine, which meant that the front wheels carried the greater part of the weight, emphasizing the totality of the metamorphosis through which the car had gone.

No longer the safe, forgiving car it used to be, the tail of the post-1974 Midget swung wide, requiring skill and tact to bring it back. To make matters worse, it became sensitive to the throttle, and lifting-off on a bend would bring the tail out very quickly, needing opposite lock to put matters right. Driving the new car fast could give the driver a very busy time indeed, for it was less predictable, less stable in a straight line and uncomfortably skittish in the wet.

The tyres were now inadequate for the extra power, with the same 145—13-inch section as before. But fortunately, there had been no meddling with the steering, and the quick, high-geared feel remained, to get drivers out of the difficulties into which the redesign might lead them.

As a genuine 100-mph car, the Midget was once again able at least to keep up with the small Fords, Fiats and Volkswagens, whose ancestors had been so slothful. The final drive remained at 3.9:1, but the adoption of the single-rail corporate Leyland gearbox meant that the 1500 engine had to drive the car through a rather wider set of ratios. Also, the axle ratio, coupled with the same-size tyres, meant that the old problem of under-gearing returned. The car's new top speed was attained beyond the red line marked on the tachometer at 6,000 rpm. Higher gearing would have improved economy, and also made the speeds in the gears higher, but the opportunity to achieve a really worthwhile

A Mark IV Midget displaying the Rostyle wheels which replaced the composite type in 1974, before the onset of the soft-nosed cars.

improvement in performance, and to get the best out of the increased power, was lost, for reasons which remain obscure. It can only be concluded that the performance was subdued in order to emphasize the differences between the Midget and Leyland's other sports cars, the MGB and the Spitfire.

With peak power reached at 5,500 rpm, and using this as the practical rev limit, first gear took the Midget 1500 to a modest 29 mph, second to 47 mph, then there was a yawning gap to third, at just under 70 mph.

Still, acceleration was better than with the previous model, even though standing starts produced axle tramp, which there had never been sufficient torque to induce before. There was even enough torque to pull the car away from 10 mph in the lowish top gear. Economy, however, suffered, making this the thirstiest Spridget in the series and, for the first time, 30 mpg was virtually unobtainable in everyday driving.

Very few of the traditional shortcomings of the car were put right in the quite extraordinary transformation, which had made a sow's ear from a perfectly good silk purse. The seats were a little more comfortable, which helped to disguise the ride — by now one of the bumpiest of any production car — yet the cockpit was as cramped as ever, and door handles roughly in line with the occupants' shoulders remained through all the re-upholsterings. The small wheel travel and high spring rates were responsible for the ride, and they could not be altered without a major redesign, although at least the old problem of bottoming was less critical. Yet there could be no excuse for retaining, until the car's dying days, the single-speed wipers, the extremely noisy hood, without even the choice of a Targa top (which made the Fiat X1/9 such a tempting alternative) or a fuel-tank filler incapable of taking a normal rate of delivery from a modern pump.

Before 1974, the car's primitiveness had been part of its charm; nobody objected to an unlined boot with the spare wheel on the floor. You used soft bags — it was not a car for going on the sort of holidays where you needed to dress-up. It did not even matter that the heater still had a hot water tap under the bonnet, while the rather heavy clutch merely emphasized the car's 'mechanicalness'. The trade-off was handling in the classic mould, with the poise and balance of a *sports* car.

Now that the poise and balance were gone, there was no reward for jack-knifing in order to get in. The gear whine merely sounded mean, and the wind noise round the hood had become irritating.

The Midget had lost its magic.

CHAPTER 5

Prototypes and specials

The Spridgets that got away

Even bearing in mind that it was the Healeys' job to produce prototypes, there was a quite bewildering number of projects connected with the Sprite, both directly and indirectly. Amongst them could be included X1, the so-called Red Bug, built by Donald Healey and Achille (Sammy) Sampietro as long ago as 1947. This was an unlovely creation which was an early attempt at a low-cost sports car.

The Healey code book went from X1 to X400, of which quite a lot never got off the drawing board, many never passed the development stage, and still more were built but never reached production. The distinction between cars intended purely for racing and derivatives which became road cars is sometimes blurred, for example in the case of the Sebring models, so they are best dealt with together.

The Sebring also appeared as a product of the Sprite support industry, which so persuaded BMC that the little car was underpriced. Numerous tuners and grp moulding manufacturers produced kits of parts for and modifications to Sprites and Midgets over the years, some of the results qualifying as separate models in their own right, such as the Arkley SS, the Speedwell cars, or the Climax-engined conversions produced by Jack Brabham.

Although strictly neither Sprites nor Midgets, two prototypes were built which might have become replacements for the model. Both were based on the Mini, and the first came on the heels of the Mini's announcement in 1959. The front-wheel-drive, transverse-engine formula, combined with the ingenious rubber springs of the Issigonis design, set new standards of handling, and MG were interested. Their stock-in-trade had always been small

sports cars, and although they had just begun making Sprites, they developed an open two/four-seater, which became known as the ADO 34.

The styling was done in the Austin studio at Longbridge, and development work went as far as trying it out with Hydrolastic suspension, which appeared on the Austin-Morris 1100 in 1962, but not on the Mini for a further two years. Sir Alec, BMC's chief engineer, remained unenthusiastic about the car, and the need for it diminished in 1961 with the introduction of the MG Midget alongside the Sprite and, later the same year, the Mini-Cooper. A more sporting open Mini would have been superfluous, and so the project was abandoned.

Another Abingdon project which never reached production was the EX 234, a front-engined car with independent Hydrolastic suspension, but this was more like a replacement for the MGB than for the Midget.

In Italy, the Sprite was produced by the *Soc. Generale per l'Industria Metallurgica e Meccanica*, in Milan, and known as the Innocenti 950 Sport. The basis of the car was pure Sprite, but the neat two-seat body was styled by Ghia and was well-received, providing a further incentive to BMC to make the change from the Mark I 'frog-eyes' to the Mark II in 1961. Innocenti had just started building BMC cars under licence, and in 1963 they introduced the 1,098-cc engine, followed by the 1,275-cc power unit in 1967.

The Mini became the basis for yet another prototype in 1970 when Rob Owen, a Longbridge styling engineer, drove a standard 1275 GT to Italy, and stayed for two months supervising a project at Michelotti. Thought of as a replacement for the

The 'Mark 1½' Sprite, photographed in the Cowley studio. The MG-designed rear is more or less as it would see production, but the tall front wings will be lowered to keep the proportions right before the body dies are made.

Midget, it was equipped with a Targa roof, in which the top panels could be put away in the boot, and a fixed rear window. As a styling exercise it was an unqualified success, but it was hand-built and heavy; it was slower than the standard 1,275-cc Cooper and it never reached production. In any case, the emission-control laws were beginning to affect the United States market, always so vital for Abingdon, and the cost of detoxing the 1,275-cc engine was prohibitive. The decision had to be taken to re-equip the Midget with the Spitfire engine which meant, effectively, a new model for 1974, so the pretty Michelotti project was abandoned.

Meanwhile, the Healeys had not been idle. When sales of the Mark II Sprite failed to achieve any real improvement over the Mark I, BMC thought that perhaps they had been wrong about the restyling after all, and that it was the price which was to blame. An economy version was laid out, with a single-carburettor engine and a Mark I bodyshell with headlamps in the wings and changes to the rear. These included fitting the spare wheel under a locking cover in the tail, TR 2-style. They saved £75 per car, and the changes led, in Geoffrey Healey's view, to a better-looking car than the Mark II. It was also lighter, but sales

improved while it was still being discussed, and so the idea of the 'Mark 1½' was dropped.

To meet an expected challenge from the Honda S800, the Healeys tested a Midget, first with a Cooper S engine, then with another engine proposed by Eddie Maher at Morris Engines. The tests, carried out at the MIRA (Motor Industry Research Association) proving ground, were set out by Geoffrey Healey in his book, *More Healeys* (Gentry Books), in which he explained that Maher's engine was an uprated Sprite power unit which would have been less costly to produce and would also have been less thirsty than the Cooper S version. As it turned out, the Honda S800 challenge was not to be sustained (tests had revealed that although its high-revving 791-cc engine had a superior output to that of the standard Spridget unit, the Japanese car's roadholding, by comparison, was atrocious) and so the need for an uprated Spridget engine largely disappeared. Geoffrey Healey also comments in his excellent book that he believes MG were none too keen on increasing the Spridget's performance, as it would then have been brought too close to that of the MGB. Nevertheless, the MIRA tests proved to be a revealing exercise in

as much as they demonstrated that Mayer's 'economy' engine was superior to the Cooper S not only in fuel consumption, but also in acceleration figures, using the same 3.9:1 axle ratio and revving to 6,300 rpm in the gears. The Mayer engine's figures are given first:

    0-30 mph 3.50/3.62 seconds
    0-40 mph 5.40/6.32 seconds
    0-50 mph 7.95/9.70 seconds
    0-60 mph 11.70/13.17 seconds
    0-70 mph 15.90/19.10 seconds
    0-80 mph 22.90/28.15 seconds
    Standing quarter-mile 18.0/18.8 seconds

There were also improvements in maximum speed, top-gear acceleration and steady-speed fuel consumption figures.

As another insurance against a slump in the sales of the Spridget, BMC commissioned the Healeys to design one possible replacement which could be called forward if the need arose. Hydrolastic suspension, based on interconnected fluid and rubber combined springs and dampers, seemed the way to go, and BMC hedged their bets with three separate projects. The Austin

Drawing Office, with their experience of transverse-engined, front-wheel-drive cars, would design one. MG at Abingdon, under Sydney Enever, would equip a Sprite with Hydrolastic suspension, and the Healeys at Warwick were to produce a two-seater with a 1,275-cc transverse engine at the rear.

Their inclination to grasp at fundamentals led the Healeys to call their car WAEC, standing for Wheel At Each Corner, a fashionable phrase used to describe cars which did not roll or sway like contemporary American models with their long overhangs. The basis was to be the subframes of the production 1100, with a Healey-designed chassis platform connecting them up. It was really a logical progression from the Mark I Sprite notion of using standard suspension, engine and transmission units and linking them together with appropriate metal.

Les Ireland designed the body with a fixed rear window and a Targa top. The rear window could be lowered electrically, making the frame effectively an open roll-over bar, thought to be necessary to meet pending US safety regulations. Vertical rear windows had become a (short-lived) fashion feature of Ford Anglias and Classics, but noise from the engine when it was open

Another Healey 'Mark 1½', this time with the wavy grille used on a number of Austin models to provide a family resemblance. Yet another version of this design had a bonnet air scoop.

Two more attempts to get rid of the frog-eyed look of the original Sprite. In this instance the headlights have been moved outboard to a conventional wing-top position, but the Mark I grille has been retained.

proved a problem when the prototype was built.

The car turned out to be heavy, and the rear engine gave the Healeys some oversteer problems to solve. Geoffrey Healey says the roadholding was leech-like, but the back broke away first, and one was never sure exactly when. The demerits turned out to be the expected conservatism of the sports car market, according to BMC, and perhaps more important, the expected cost of such a car. The Austin and MG designs were similarly dropped.

On the Healeys' initiative, dating back to 1959, shortly after the introduction of the Mark I Sprite, three prototypes were built with Coventry Climax engines. They wanted to market a car in parallel with the BMC Sprite to be called the Super Sprite, with an 1,100-cc Climax single-overhead-camshaft four-cylinder engine. Based on a Mark I platform, XQHS, as it was known, was eminently pretty, but BMC killed it on the grounds that it would not be in their best interests to have the Healeys working with outside engine manufacturers.

However, no such inhibitions affected conversion specialists such as Jack Brabham, who fitted 1,216-cc Coventry Climax FWE units in Sprites and Midgets from 1962 onwards. The

Climax was a neat fit, and not only was it some 40 lb (18.1 kg) lighter, but it gave 80 per cent more power than the standard unit. The 0-50 mph time was halved and top speed went up by 25 per cent to around 112 mph.

BMC always had a curiously ambivalent attitude to racing. The Donald Healey Motor Company had an allocation of money towards their racing programme, and BMC also supported the Cooper Car Company's activities in Formula Junior (leading, incidentally, to the launching of the career of a new, young Scottish driver, Jackie Stewart). Abingdon's racing programme, however, had to be *sub rosa*. From BMC's point of view, their policy made sense because, as many others had found before them, farming out a racing programme meant they would always be in a position to acknowledge success, while always having somebody else to blame, or disown, in the event of failure.

Nonetheless, the MG Development Department built three of what were probably the best-developed Spridgets ever. There was talk at the time (1962) that the cars were possible production prototypes. The two-plus-two body style was proving popular, and although the MGB GT was still two years away the market

Super Sprite. The Healeys' own project for a successor to the Sprite was XQHS, the 1,100-cc Coventry Climax-engined version which they intended to sell in small numbers as an up-market derivative. The single-overhead-camshaft engine gave this 1959 car such a vivid performance, however, that BMC forbade its production, fearing competition with their established MG and Austin-Healey range. The car was based on Sprite presswork, with a body by Les Ireland.

was demanding a quieter, more refined product. Motorways were having their effect, draughty two-seaters were meeting a certain amount of resistance, and a closed Midget was certainly worthy of study. Secret prototypes were all concentrating on refinement, with engaging ploys such as the Targa roof.

These GT Midgets, as they became known, were legitimate attempts to test out the water for a production version, yet they were more truly a means of getting Abingdon into racing by Dick Jacobs' back door. Jacobs was an MG dealer in Essex, with a long history of competition at the wheel of MGs right up to the 1955 Le Mans race, when he was badly injured in one of the prototype MGAs. He had not been involved in the disastrous accident in which over 80 spectators died, but the Le Mans disaster, together with his long, painful recovery, worried the MG management about taking part in racing for many years to come.

Probably the most numerous Spridget derivatives, certainly in the early years, were the many known as Sebring Sprites, which reached large enough numbers to be recognized by the FIA as a separate model.

Consideration of the Sprite's Sebring career is given in the

chapter on racing, but the road model known as the Sebring was introduced by the Healeys at Warwick as a lightweight version of the Mark I, with the engine modified with the current range of Healey Speed Equipment. In effect, it was a package deal of all the conversion equipment Healey sold as separate items. The prettier Sebring bodywork was a later introduction by John Sprinzel, who had worked for the Healeys in London. As with the subsequent BMC Special Tuning arrangement, the Healeys' Sebring specification altered the car in stages, but the 'full house' car was worked on fairly comprehensively.

The engine was the first item to be treated. The standard 948-cc capacity was increased to 995 cc by boring-out, and everything was carefully balanced. The inlet ports were smoothed-out, as were the combustion chambers, and high-compression, solid-skirt pistons were fitted to raise the compression ratio to 11:1. A sports camshaft with special bearings and a sports coil were added and the carburettors were replaced with 1½-inch units, each with its own fuel pump. Special inlet and exhaust manifolds were used, with two tailpipes all the way through the silencer. The result was 80 bhp at 7,000 rpm.

This special EX 219 Sprite was built by the Abingdon Development Department, using much standard material, but with a body based on the famous Goldie Gardner and Eyston record-breakers. Here is Tommy Wisdom, at the wheel, talking to Alec Hounslow of the Development Department.

Tommy Wisdom has little room to spare with the lid of the 'bubble top' cockpit closed. The car was taken to the Utah salt flats in the USA soon afterwards, where Wisdom, Gus Ehrman and Ed Leavens took 15 International Class G records between 50 kilometres and 12 hours at speeds up to almost 147 mph.

A competition clutch with nine springs replaced the standard item, along with a close-ratio needle-roller gearbox, specially strong half-shafts and sealed wheel bearings. The suspension was basically unchanged, except for the addition of an anti-roll bar and stiffer front springs. Armstrong adjustable dampers were fitted at the rear, together with stronger leaf springs. The track was increased by the use of centre-lock 60-spoke wire wheels, and Girling disc brakes of 8½-in diameter helped contain the greatly increased performance.

The body was panelled in aluminium, in the well-proportioned fixed-head coupe style that made the car look not unlike a Mark 1 Lotus Elite. The bonnet was moulded in grp and hinged at the front, and while cars intended for rallying needed to keep the steel bulkhead and wheelarches, racing Sebrings could be further lightened by replacing more panels with aluminium and grp. The weight could be reduced to about 11 cwt (559 kg), giving the car a lively performance with a top speed on a 4.8:1 axle of around 105 mph and a standing-quarter time of 17 sec.

Record-breaking was still used as a means of gaining publicity in 1959, although how many sports car buyers it impressed

Cockpit of EX 219, which was based on Sprite floor pressings, with instruments confined to rev counter and pressure and temperature gauges. The 'flattened' steering wheel rim, of course, was to provide the necessary leg clearance during runs which called for comparatively little steering wheel movement.

remains a matter for debate. At the same time as MG were taking EX 181, the teardrop-shaped record car with which Stirling Moss had reached 245 mph in 1957, for a second visit to Utah, another car, EX 219, was built. Labelled as an Austin-Healey Sprite, it was really nothing of the sort, having a body resembling the famous Goldie Gardner MG, and a chassis like that of EX 179, which was a prototype MGA. EX 179/219 had been to Utah before; in 1957 David Ash and Tommy Wisdom had averaged 118.13 mph for 12 hours with a 948-cc A35/Morris Minor engine at an astonishing 49.8 miles per gallon (5.6 litres per 100 km). With a Shorrock supercharger, Phil Hill covered a flying mile at 142.47 mph, and the car gained no less than nine International and 56 American National records.

Now, it returned as an Austin-Healey, with right-hand drive, once again in Shorrock supercharged form, ostensibly to 'attempt

an endurance test of the Austin-Healey Sprite, BMC 950-cc four-cylinder A-Series engine. The engine and gearbox are in most respects quite standard, such as cylinder-block, head, crankshaft and all other details. The few special parts, such as pistons, valves, valve springs and clutch . . . can be obtained through BMC Service Ltd, for competition tuning of the standard Sprite. To obtain the additional power required for these high speeds, an ordinary Shorrock low-pressure, belt-driven supercharger kit is fitted. This gives a manifold pressure of 6 to 7 lb per square inch (.42 to .49 kg-cm) and the engine will produce 78 bhp at 5,500 rpm or 86 bhp at 6,000. For the 12-hour record, we shall be using approximately 70 bhp at 5,400 rpm for 135 mph, using a 2.88:1 rear-axle ratio. So that we may also attempt a short-distance sprint record at maximum speed, a spare engine is available, with a slightly higher compression ratio (otherwise

At one stage there was the possibility of a two-seater sports car, based on Mini components, which would have replaced the front-engined, rear-driven Spridgets, but the concept caused considerable controversy within the heirarchy of BMC and the project was dropped. This is how the MG version might have looked, although there was more than one variant on the ADO 34 theme, as the project was coded.

The Austin-Healey Sprite version of the Mini-based sports car was conceived in this form and was given the code number ADO 36. Mini designer Sir Alec Issigonis was violently opposed to his 'ultimate packaging' concept being dissipated in a space-wasting two-seater.

identical to the 12-hour engine) developing 98 bhp at 6,500 rpm, with which it is hoped we shall attain 145/150 mph'.

The 'Sprite' broke a number of International Class G records, from 50 km at 145.56 mph to 2,000 km at 138.86 mph, driven by Tommy Wisdom, Ed Leavens and Gus Ehrman — a creditable achievement, but not very convincing to the sports car enthusiast who now recognized what a specialized business record-breaking was, and how little resemblance the cars bore to anything he might drive on the road.

He was rather more aware of the small concerns marketing parts and components, engine conversions and body panels with which he could alter his Sprite or Midget. Some remained in the business throughout the model's 21-year history; others came and went.

One which has been sold since about 1970 is the Arkley SS, a kit of parts which offers owners of late-Mark Midgets the chance to turn back the clock; it can also prolong the active life of older Spridgets, provided they have sound centre-sections. For a relatively small outlay on plastics nose and tail sections, any Mark of Spridget can be turned into a fair imitation of a Mark I Sprite

This Arkley conversion has been given a rather strange appearance by its oversize wheels and tyres, but these otherwise very attractive little sports cars have given a new lease of life to many a damaged or bodily corroded Spridget.

with flared wings and a cropped tail. The cost does not end with the bodywork, of course. The Arkley is incomplete without wide wheels and tyres, and the painting and finishing have also to be taken into account.

Lenham and Wilson-Spratt were only two of the names from the Spridget support industry, altering and modifying cars for the road or for rallying. The engine-conversion specialists were legion, from the amazingly efficient and effective Daniel Richmond, to many that were more expensive, more elaborate and much less good. The little car's enthusiastic owners tended to be individualists who wanted their Spridget to be different, and except perhaps for those with post-1974 Midgets, whose room for manoeuvre was necessarily limited, many of them contrived to do just that.

CHAPTER 6

Sprites and Midgets in competition

From autotests to endurance rallies and races

Works participation in motor racing at the time of the Sprite's announcement was inhibited by the fact that Lance Macklin's Austin-Healey 100S had been involved in the 1955 Le Mans disaster; the Healeys did not expose the name in a major European race for some time afterwards. However, the small Sprite was a different matter, and soon after its introduction, following the example of private owners, a team was entered in the Alpine Rally.

This was a familiar event for Donald Healey. He had endorsed the Alpine since the 1930s as a proving ground for his Invictas, Rileys and Triumphs. He believed firmly that the resulting publicity was an encouragement to sales; sports car buyers would surely be convinced by sports car successes.

For the Sprite, it was an impressive debut. John Sprinzel and Willy Cave led three cars to a convincing first, second and third in the under-1,000-cc class for Groups 2 and 6. Less than half the 56 starters finished the course. It was the first of many such victories for Sprinzel, who had gained a reputation as a successful tuner and racer of Austin A35s. The same weekend, a journalist on the staff of *The Motor,* John Anstice-Brown, gained the Sprite's first race victory when he won the Leinster Trophy, a two-heat handicap event at Dunboyne, in Ireland. The Sprite was launched encouragingly on its competition career.

The value of competition as a sales medium was, in the Sprite's case, doubtful. So far as Britain was concerned, its successes, while creditable, probably sold fewer cars than did the tangible and recognizable virtues of the car. With the exception of Sprinzel's astonishing success in the 'Liège', most buyers were probably more impressed with the handling, the economy and the

fun that could be had with the car. Only class victories could be expected from 1,000 cc, and they were not very impressive to the run-of-the-mill enthusiast. In rallies, Sprites were destined to be swamped by bigger, stronger cars for the principal awards. Record-breaking was no longer taken seriously, and despite a good deal of follow-up advertising, the performances at Le Mans and Sebring may have been significant in export markets where the customers had a hazy knowledge of what was what in international racing, but to the sports car buff in Britain they were class awards, and nothing more.

To them, the Sprite was essentially a miniature, affordable scale model of the 250 TR Ferraris, Aston Martin DBR1s, or the soon-to-arrive 'Birdcage' Maseratis. It was a car with which to have fun in local night navigation trials and gymkhanas, particularly the latter, because it was so manoeuvrable, light and precise that for a time nothing else stood a chance. It looked the part, and handled like a mildly roadworthy racer. Yet it was not one, at least not in its virgin production state of tune.

Having said that, it was surprising how close the racing Sprites remained to their production counterparts. Indeed, the domestic enthusiast might have been more impressed had he known. What he refused to believe were the implications in BMC's publicity that Sprites were winning Le Mans and doing 150 mph at Utah. Yet while he was sceptical about the claims, the truth was that the Sprites which were achieving class victories had far more production items aboard than their constant rivals, the Fiat-Abarths.

That first Alpine Rally performance was never matched, although Tommy Wisdom and Jack Hay repeated their second in

The motoring press gather round one of the soon-to-retire team of Sprites during the Alpine Rally, in June 1960. This is the Tommy Wisdom/Jack Hay car, and while Hay, wearing a soft hat, peers beneath the uplifted bonnet, Wisdom, in peaked cap, talks to Courtenay Edwards, facing the camera, Harold Nockolds, facing Wisdom in plastic raincoat, and a smartly suited Basil Cardew — a gathering composed entirely of past and future Chairmen of the Guild of Motoring Writers.

The ill-fated Sprite entered for Le Mans by Ecurie Ecosse with past winner Ninian Sanderson and newcomer Bill McKay, who was seriously injured when he crashed the car early in the evening. The following DB Panhards finished 20th and 18th, respectively.

class the following year, and also managed second in the GT category to a DB Panhard. Sprinzel and Cave took the same position in 1961, and John Williamson and David Hiam did so yet again in 1962.

By this time, rallies were becoming altogether more punishing and demanding affairs, yet it was on just such an event that the Sprite scored two of its most meritorious successes. This was the Liège-Rome-Liège, which had not yet reached as far as Sofia, and really started and finished at the Belgian resort of Spa.

The 'Liège', as it would always be known, was one of the toughest motoring events ever. Organized by the Royal Motor Union over 3,000-odd miles, it regularly produced no more than a handful of finishers after five days and nights at racing speeds over the most appalling surfaces in Europe. The history of the Marathon de la Route went back to 1931, but it was in the 1950s and 1960s that it came to represent all that was best in long-distance rallying. By the late-1950s, traffic and speed restrictions in the Alps and Dolomites had pressed it into Yugoslavia in search of its traditional, testing terrain, and it gained such a reputation that merely reaching the finish was regarded as an achievement.

John Sprinzel and Stuart Turner won their class in 1959, finishing eighth out of 14 survivors from an entry of 104. The following year, Sprinzel, partnered this time by John Patten, won the class again, in the smallest car to finish, and was placed third out of 13 cars which struggled back to Belgium after the gruelling route.

Sprinzel's remarkable results were achieved in a privately entered car, while the BMC cup brimmed over with the success of Austin-Healey 3000s finishing first, fifth and 10th and winning the team prize. Built and run by the BMC Competitions Department at Abingdon, adjacent to, but administratively separate from MG, the Big Healey's success, if anything, enhanced that of the Sprite. In any case, Sprinzel's triumph was probably worth more in prestige and sales than all the special models built for the Targa Florio, Le Mans and Sebring put together.

Even two second places in the RAC Rally were not very convincing in 1959 and 1960. Still, together with the two class victories of Tommy Gold/Mike Hughes and John Sprinzel/

John Sprinzel, with hands on hips, confers with Tommy Wisdom on the 1959 Monte Carlo Rally. Sprinzel, co-driving with Willy Cave, finished 14th overall and third in class, while Wisdom, sharing his car with Douglas Johns, was 63rd overall and fifth in class. The other two cars of Baxter/Reece and Wilson-Spratt/Bayliss both retired.

Two of the successful Sprites on the 1958 Alpine Rally. Tommy Wisdom and Jack Hay finished 19th overall and second in class in YAC 104, while the car in front, the famous first PMO 200, was driven by John Sprinzel and Willy Cave into 15th place, winning their class. A third car, driven by Brookes and Wells-West, completed the class hat-trick for Sprites.

A group of National Servicemen enjoying the very essence of Sprite competition in April 1960. They are watching a private entrant tackling a tough hill on the Land's End Trial and — judging by the blurred rear wheel and stationary front — not making a great deal of progress.

A thoughtful Marcus Chambers, BMC's team manager, Tommy Wisdom and Donald Healey ponder on their works cars' performance on an Alpine Rally. The grille of this car, with Jack Hay at the wheel, has been opened out to allow in extra cooling air.

John Sprinzel, with his hardtop-equipped Sprite PMO 200, heading for a class victory in the 1958 Alpine Rally on the outskirts of Barcelonnette.

Richard Bensted-Smith (soon to be editor of *The Motor)* they probably impressed the enthusiasts taking part in club events. The RAC Rally, of course, was at a watershed in its history, with special stages soon to be introduced. The classic event was about to change from being a curious mixture of night-navigation trial and sea-front gymkhana, to become the rally of the forests in which the long overnight road sections would become relatively unimportant.

The BMC Competitions Department never formally developed the Sprite, preferring the opportunity offered by the Big Healey of outright wins, clearly beyond the smaller car's capabilities.

Nor did the Sprite have the potential of the Mini-Cooper. Most of its real achievements were the result of the efforts of private owners, sometimes helped in one way or another by the works. They took part in most of the major international events of the time, Sprinzel and Cave gaining a third place in their class in the 1959 Monte Carlo Rally, Wilson-Spratt and Bayliss a fifth the following year, and Sprinzel and Christabel Carlisle a fourth in 1962, when the class was won by a new MG Midget driven by Peter Riley and Mike Hughes. The following year the rallying

clergymen, Rupert Jones and Philip Morgan, once again scored a class win in the Monte, but managed only 69th in the general classification. Douglas Wilson-Spratt was amongst the most successful rally entrants with his distinctive and well-prepared cars, but except for the Circuit of Ireland, the Spridget tended to drop out of international road events after the early-1960s.

On the racing side, the Healeys' subsidy from BMC was put to good use, in particular at Sebring and Le Mans. It was also used on forays to the Targa Florio which, while it was a classic event in quite an epic style, somehow failed to impress the grass-roots British enthusiast. It was regarded as rather a remote affair, and the Targa Sprites, mostly quite unlike production cars to look at, were never considered as anything but disguised racing cars. In the late-1950s that sort of thing still mattered — it was still somehow 'not quite cricket' to take a sports car to a race on a trailer. The suspicion — unfair as it turned out — that racing Sprites were far removed from production models was never allayed by the BMC promotional machine, and the value of such success as the cars were to achieve in the Targa was largely lost.

The Warwick-built Targa Florio cars were prefixed TFR (for

A Le Mans-type start at Sebring in 1960, when the Mark I Sprites scored a class victory over the Turners, one of which, car number 6, has got away briskly.

Although the Sprite was becoming outclassed in international events by 1962, John Williamson and David Hiam managed a commendable 20th place overall and second in class on the Alpine Rally.

This is one of the works cars which were built for the 1962 Sebring 3 Hours GT race, but seen here in private hands tackling the famous Prescott hill-climb in May 1964.

Knobbly rear tyres are fitted to this Mark II Sprite in an effort to find some much needed grip on a wet and slippery hill during the 1964 Land's End Trial.

Targa Florio Race) and number 1 was built for 1959. The drivers were Tommy Wisdom and Bernard Cahier, distinguished journalists who could be relied upon to secure the maximum publicity in Britain and France — at least in the papers for which they wrote. The engine acquired a sports camshaft, polished ports and 1½-in carburettors. Disc brakes still lay in the future, but to help stop the little racer on the 45-mile circuit round Sicily, 8-in Austin A40 drums were fitted at the front. Any nuts that might come loose were wire-locked and the team set off for the Mediterranean, as always, driving the race car.

Preparation turned out to be satisfactory, although the throttle cable broke in the race, but the management seems to have been a little haphazard and refuelling arrangements depended on a plastic canister in the car, which burst after two laps. The best that could be achieved was 17th overall and sixth in the class.

It was 1964 before TFR2 was built. This was a lightweight open car, the first of the rather more special Targa Florio cars, and it looked completely different from TFR1, which had the standard bodywork. Incidentally, this was the first Sprite to be equipped with half-elliptic springs. An alloy body with a fashionable raised tail and spoiler was built on to a standard chassis platform. It looked gratifyingly like a miniature Ferrari, but one wonders if there was any real advantage to be gained from making it appear so different from the Sprite-in-the-street.

Remembering the nonsense with the plastic container in 1959, a large fuel tank was built-in to allow three laps before refuelling. There was a roll-over hoop and, for driving to Sicily, a Mini laminated screen. During practice there was trouble with half-shaft breakages, and another from the same faulty batch put the car out of the race when Paddy Hopkirk was driving.

One problem with TFR2 was too much understeer, so TFR3 was built with yet another body in which the fuel tank was moved further to the rear and lowered, and the inclination of the rear springs was reduced. The substantial roll cage was ostensibly for safety reasons, but it also played a useful role in stiffening the structure and making this one of the best-handling Sprites ever.

Stirling Moss' 1962 Sebring car taking part on the 1963 Nurburgring 1,000-Kilometres race, when it was shared by Clive Baker and Christabel Carlisle. It was running behind two Porsche Carreras when the English girl took over, and after following them for a couple of laps she passed them both and never looked back. Hedges and Martyn finished 13th in the same race, driving an MG Midget, and Foster and Greene were 15th in a similar car, two places ahead of the Baker/Carlisle Sprite.

Geoffrey Healey always regarded TFR3 as the best of all the special Sprites and he considered it perfectly matched to the Targa course, being quick to turn into a corner and with lots of traction.

Any chance of doing well in the race, however, was spoiled by brake trouble, but Rauno Aaltonen and Clive Baker finished 15th overall and second in their class. Afterwards, TFR3 was used on the road, to Geoffrey Healey's delight, and later it was converted into TFR4, a coupe version for the 1966 race. An accident, and yet another broken half-shaft, produced another disappointment, however, and only 16th overall and third place in the class.

Undaunted, TFR5 duly appeared for 1967, with Girling light-alloy caliper brakes and a 1,293-cc engine. A pedestrian put paid to this car's chances, Clive Baker crashing as a result of a race-time jaywalker.

For 1968, it was decided that the Targa cars ought to look like road cars after all, so a production Mark IV Sprite was modified a good deal and fitted with a 1,293-cc dry-sump engine, five-speed gearbox and Minilite wheels. Once again the drivers were Rauno Aaltonen and Clive Baker, and the car went well, lying second in class and actually overtaking the works MGB before the head gasket failed and it boiled its water away. The interesting Sprite Special of Jack Wheeler and Martin Davidson, who had been sixth in the class the year before with a Sprite, was no more fortunate. This was a private entry, a specially built Lotus hybrid, featuring Elan suspension and chassis backbone grafted on to a Sprite floor platform. Unfortunately, the Lotus rear suspension mounting broke on the bumps and humps of the Sicilian circuit

One of the racing coupes in course of preparation in the Healeys' workshops, converted from an old cinema at Coten End. This is a 1964 version, with a tubular roof structure welded to a Sprite floorpan, before the wind tunnel tests caused the rear-end shape to be changed.

and the car retired.

The final year of the Healeys' sorties to the Targa Florio was to have been 1969, with TFR7, a wedge-shaped open car with a cut-off tail. It had been modelled on the Le Mans coupes, and its creators were so pleased with it, resplendent in its polished aluminium, that they never painted it. Alas, the car was completed just in time to suffer from British Leyland's competition budget cuts, and it never took part in the race. Instead, it was sold to Ed Bussey, the Florida MG and Austin distributor.

In the United States, Sprites fared somewhat better in the races created by Alex Ulmann on the runways and perimeter track of the former Hendricks Air Force Base. Sebring dated from 1950, the 12-Hours races being instituted there in 1952 and gaining

world championship status the following year as the Sebring Grand Prix of Endurance.

The American dealers were instrumental in getting a team of Sprites entered in 1959, following several years' successful participation with Austin-Healey 100 and 100-Six models. But the American end of BMC was also keen for the team control to remain in the hands of the BMC Competitions Department, and for the sake of peace amongst the importers, Warwick had to agree.

With the prospect of a long, tough race, four standard Sprites were given the designation ST200 and provided with engines in only a moderate state of tune. A power output of 57 bhp was considered sufficient, giving a top speed of 98 mph, but for a race that was always hard on brakes the cars were equipped with the

recently homologated Dunlop 'light car' disc brakes, which were really only available for these works cars and gave the promise of 12 hours' racing without a pad change.

Sprite gearboxes were often troublesome in racing, but despite some problems, the three race cars finished first, second and third in their class, although the highest-placed was only 31st in the general classification.

A Four-Hours race for the smaller cars took place at the following year's Sebring meeting, for which the first Targa Florio car, TFR1, was eligible. The engine had been modified by Weslake to obtain a little more power, and the car was driven by no less than Stirling Moss, then at the height of his brilliant career.

It was a case of Moss' skill against the more powerful twin-cam Abarths, a favourable equation except for the rate at which Moss used up tyres. It was not his fault; the problem simply had not arisen with slower drivers. The Sprite duly won its class, but a rather long stop for a change of tyres had allowed an Abarth into the overall lead, and Moss' car went on to finish second. It was probably the Sprite's best ever opportunity for a major

international race victory, and it had been missed, although a further class victory in the 12-Hours race was some compensation.

Moss was in the team again the following year, in which the frog-eyed Sprites had bodies in glass-reinforced plastic moulded from the production car. Now, at last, some cunning was being used to relate the racing cars to the road versions. In the Four-Hours race the Sprites came second, fourth, fifth, sixth, seventh and eighth overall after once again giving second-best to the Abarths. In the 12-Hours event the Sprites gained second and third in a combined 1,150-cc and 1,000-cc class won by a Lola-Climax.

The successes of the Abarths and the Sprites were reflected in the entry for the 1962 Four-Hours. Of the 29 starters, there were 13 Abarths and 10 Sprites, including the works cars to be driven by Moss, Pedro Rodriguez, Innes Ireland and Steve McQueen. An Abarth driven by Bruce McLaren won the race, but by a narrow margin after Moss had had to stop for fuel with a quarter of an hour to go. McQueen very nearly won his class in the 12-Hours until a main bearing cap broke.

For the 1963 short race, one of the cars was badge-engineered to become an MG and was driven by Graham Hill. The new limited-slip differentials failed within the first five laps, although the Abarths were beaten for a class victory in the 12-Hours race by John Colgate and Clive Baker in the 1,098-cc coupe. The same pair managed it again the following year, despite a failing oil pump in the closing stages.

In 1965, the Le Mans coupe was used by Aaltonen and Baker to win the class and finish 15th, while Paddy Hopkirk was only three places behind with one of the aluminium-bodied older cars. The car which Andrew Hedges and Roger Mac drove to win their class in the GT category was a Midget and over the next three years BMC and Leyland made strenuous efforts to shift the

publicity spotlight on to the MG marque as the end of the line for the Austin-Healey approached.

Class victories continued, however, in what had become almost a preserve of the cars, now with 1293-cc fuel-injection engines. Even after works participation had ceased, the Ring Free Oil Racing Team cars carried on the class-winning tradition.

The Healeys returned to Le Mans in 1960 with a rather hastily built 996-cc car, which used a Falcon glass-fibre bodyshell with a rather tall windscreen demanded by the regulations. The result was a victory in the relatively unimportant class for 1,000-cc cars and a disputed fifth place in the Index of Thermal Efficiency, which Geoffrey Healey believed should have been fourth.

The more lasting result was a commitment to Le Mans for most

John Colgate and Paul Hawkins shared this first works coupe in the 1961 Le Mans race, but it dropped out of the race with valve trouble after eight hours. Here it is back in Britain running wheel-to-wheel with a Shelby Cobra in the wet.

The Sprite of Sir John Whitmore and Bob Olthoff in hot pursuit of the second-placed Ferrari GTO through the Esses at Le Mans in 1963. However, Olthoff was to be injured when he crashed in the car soon after one o'clock the following morning.

A shorter race than expected. Early in the 1964 Le Mans race, the Sprite shared by Clive Baker and Bill Bradley is in close company with a Triumph Spitfire (49) and a Deep Sanderson (42), but both the Sprite's rivals were to drop out within the first two hours.

of the following eight years and the construction of a number of Le Mans coupes. These started with ST 461, using the understructure of the 1960 car, but replacing the Falcon body with a closed fastback based on XQHS, the extremely pretty Super Sprite prototype, which the Healeys had wanted to put on the market with a Coventry Climax engine.

A Manx-tailed coupe was built for 1963, but was crashed by Bob Olthoff and replaced by another with a body built on the 1964 Targa Florio car body buck. For a small car, however, aerodynamics were a persistent problem. Accordingly, the 1964 Le Mans and Targa Florio cars were subjected to wind-tunnel tests by the Austin Research Department, resulting in a number of improvements. Critical areas were discovered round the windscreen pillars and the way the windows were moulded into the body sides. For stability, the roof peak was kept as close as possible to the front of the car, with a gentle slope towards the back, while a full undertray was needed, together with a smaller radiator opening.

The result was an altogether smoother profile, and an extra 10 mph or so to give a top speed of well over 140 mph. The

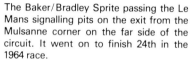

The Baker/Bradley Sprite passing the Le Mans signalling pits on the exit from the Mulsanne corner on the far side of the circuit. It went on to finish 24th in the 1964 race.

Following the 1964 Le Mans race, Doc Weaving, at Austin, put the racing Sprites through some wind tunnel tests, and the result was this more slippery shape, which was used for the 1965 race, when Paul Hawkins and John Rhodes finished 12th. Here, the car is being track-tested for the magazine *Motor Racing*.

highly developed Sprites now suffered from the attentions of the same French scrutineers, who had so upset Colin Chapman when his slippery and efficient cars took part. They even complained about the paintwork of the cars, which were now capable of 147 mph on the Mulsanne Straight, and they exasperated the team, but were unable to prevent them finishing 12th overall and cleaning-up their class against the French opposition. It was the best result at Le Mans, although unfortunately a second car blew-up.

Lucas petrol-injection was used in subsequent years, and the engine was raised in capacity to 1,293 cc. Front-rear brake balancing was brought in, and a special gearbox, based on the MGB model, with a special housing at the rear to fit a fifth gear, was used in an effort to cure the cars' transmission weaknesses. With 120 bhp there were difficulties over cracking cylinder-heads, which were met by Tuftriding treatment, lowering the compression to 11.9:1 and limiting the revs to 7,000 rpm. The result was *The Motor* Trophy for best-placed British car in 1967, and two more 15th places, but once again the British Leyland budget closed the proceedings, and the active, official competition

life of the Sprite came to an end.

In view of Dick Jacobs' long and distinguished career as an MG driver prior to his serious Le Mans accident (referred to in the previous chapter), it was appropriate that he should be the person to take MG back on to the track, this time as an entrant. Two of the three GT Midgets built by the MG Development Department were assigned to him on loan, and he engaged Andrew Hedges and Alan Foster as regular drivers. The cars, which remained the property of the works, were taken to many successes, including a class win and third overall in the 1963 *Autosport* Championship, and a class first and second in the 1964 Nurburgring 1000 Kilometres. The third car went to Scottish enthusiast John Milne, and was raced with conspicuous success for many years.

The existing platform chassis was used, with a hand-beaten aluminium body mounted with a combination of rivets and epoxy-resin adhesive. The shape was developed in the wind tunnel, and the weight saving over the standard Midget amounted to 324 lb (147 kg) in a total all-up weight of 1,242 lb (563 kg). Disc brakes pre-dated the production car's by a matter of months,

The Dick Jacobs Midgets remained competitive for some years after official works participation in racing had ceased. The team made a clean sweep of the 1,300-cc prototype class in the 1964 Nurburgring 1,000-kilometres race when one car was equipped with a 1,275-cc BMC engine and the other a very hot 1,293-cc unit with dry-sump lubrication. Driven by Andrew Hedges and Keith Greene and by Chris Martyn and Alan Foster, they finished ahead of the Sprite of Clive Baker and Bill Bradley in a class which also included Marcos, Alpine-Renault, Rene Bonnet and Diva opposition.

the suspension was a modified version of standard, and the engine began as a tuned 979 cc unit giving 75 bhp, was later enlarged to 995 cc, then 1,139 cc and eventually 1,293 cc. The curious sizes came about as they represented the largest increases in capacity of the 948-cc, 1,098-cc and 1,275-cc engines which were permitted under racing regulations.

There was a certain amount of Formula Junior engine in the little power units, with a twin-choke Weber carburettor, four-branch exhaust and close attention to the combustion chambers and porting. The gears were close-ratio, but the standard 4.875:1

axle was retained. The suspension alterations included higher-rate springs, an anti-roll bar, competition Armstrong shock absorbers at the front and variable-setting Armstrongs at the back, with the normal quarter-elliptic springs.

These special GT versions of the Midget, however, were to be overtaken by the opposition in major events well before the end of the 1960s. The Spridget's competition successes were rarely in the big arena, anyway, as the car was out of its depth, except for that one highlight of Sprinzel's in the 'Liège'. It was much more at home in the hands of the private owners who ran it in every

Modsports racing at Longridge, with an assortment of Sprites being driven by Gary Wilson, Peter Green and David Abram caught by the camera of Peter McFadyen.

Michael Maule's Modsports Mark I Sprite, photographed here by Colin Bicknell, is a far cry from the modest-looking standard product with flared wheelarches covering its racing wheels and tyres.

kind of event from production car trials to rallycross, and from club sprints to the 1000-Kilometres at the Nurburgring.

These days, the sustained efforts and enthusiasm of the MG and Austin-Healey clubs keep the Spridgets in competition, while in the United States they are campaigned in Class F production racing. Yet the most astonishing development has been the Production and Modified Sports categories in Britain. The range of changes which every Mark of Sprite and Midget has seen in these classes makes the racing cars created by the works seem tame indeed by comparison.

In the mid-Sixties, marque racing gave way to Special Sports, then in 1969 to Modified Sports (Modsports), the Spridget fitting neatly into the 1,150 to 1,500-cc class. Based on the standard chassis of what must have been a road car, and keeping the side elevation or silhouette of the original, the result is an array of

Sprite-looking cars which reach speeds of which their chassis builders never dreamed. Spridgets, at the time of writing, hold the lap records at five British circuits.

Very few modifications are allowed in Production Sports Car racing (Prodsports) beyond safety measures, while the engines are only permitted to be 'blueprinted', which means virtually standard within manufacturers' tolerances. The classes are laid down on the principle of equivalent performance, and in category C the Spridgets reign almost supreme. At the time of writing they hold the lap record on no less than 12 British circuits — nearly a clean sweep.

Most important of all, whatever the category, the car maintains the principle laid down by its creators, namely of providing sport at a price which should not deter the most impecunious of competition drivers.

CHAPTER 7

Buying a Spridget

The choice, the examination and the road test

It will be many years before maintenance, servicing and restoration work on the Spridget becomes problematical. It may even never happen. Unlike many cars which became classics, spares for Spridgets are plentiful for the same reason that the car was conceived in the first place; so many of the parts were in production for far more numerous saloon models. Unique components were generally of such simplicity that, should they be unobtainable, they can usually be made quite easily. Almost the only Mark I item impossible to get hold of or manufacture seems to be the rubber floor covering. Sets turn up from time to time in some corner of a forgotten parts store, but new ones are unlikely to be turned out owing to the cost of the necessary dies. Most restorers of early cars are forced to follow the example of many early owners and fit carpets.

Almost everything else is obtainable either off the BL shelf (in some cases modified) or through one of the specialist parts suppliers in the UK and North America. There are, moreover, MG and Austin-Healey clubs throughout the world capable of directing restorers to sources of material and advising on the finer points of the work, or even short-cuts. The Sprite Register estimated the number of cars surviving 10 years after the last of the 130,000 or so were made at about 10,000. Well over 200 Mark Is were then on the Register, probably only a fraction of those in existence.

Prices of mint-condition Mark I Sprites rose as they became scarcer, really good or well-restored examples commanding high premiums to more than keep their original value, even allowing for inflation. For the most part, however, the relatively large numbers that survive from later Marks can be expected to hold down values. This does not mean they will remain cheap indefinitely, but steep rises in the prices of classics tend to reflect supply and demand, just like any other commodity, together with an ingredient created by the cost of restoration. Even starting from the ground up, the cost of building a Spridget from spares and built-up parts is never going to be anything like starting from scratch and making, for example, a replica D-Type Jaguar, or a GTO Ferrari.

So while the advice to, 'Invest in land, because they aren't making any more of it . . .' held good for Spridgets the moment the last one rolled off the line at the end of 1979, they are unlikely ever to be so profitable. They are unlikely to attain the inflated values reached by T-series MGs, for example, so many of which were written-off or scrapped before the nostalgia boom and the effects of legislation signalled the end of the motor car's second Vintage era.

Too many Spridgets remain for scarcity to gain them much value, and owners are now reluctant to write them off through decay, or break them up for spares now that the real worth of old cars has become so widely recognized. Its quick identification as a classic worth preserving is likely to keep Spridget prices within reach of enthusiasts, a fitting position in its 'after-life' for a car which was built as a means of supplying the less well-off with sports-car motoring.

The most likely growth area for Spridget restorers lies in the production of replica racers, such as the Dick Jacobs Midgets, from ageing hulls, or 'de-Federalizing' post-1974 rubber-bumpered cars.

The ease and cheapness (again a relative term) with which they can be repaired and restored will also help to ensure that plenty of Spridgets remain on the road — a further price depressant. As a result, Spridgets cannot be recommended as cars for the investor or speculator, which is perhaps a good thing. Cars with specific and verifiable histories, or altogether exceptional low-mileage and original-condition examples apart, they cannot be expected to gain in value at anything like the rate of Ferraris or the like, at least not for several years.

There is every incentive to keep a Spridget as a 'live' classic, which can be used and enjoyed without affecting its value, unlike some expensive museum pieces, whose chief quality lies in unblemished originality. So long as Spridgets remain plentiful, easily maintainable and relatively cheap, the proportion of value lost through being high-mileage or non-original will remain affordable.

The foregoing considerations no longer apply, however, to the Mark I Sprite. This has joined the T-series MG as a car which should not be run for fun if its value is important. Initially, it turned out to be extremely resistant to body corrosion, many pristine examples still being obtainable 10 years after they were built (proportionately fewer Minis survived as long). This was a tribute to the design of the chassis platform and the quality of the preparation and paintwork of the early cars, but after 20 years or more it has become a different story. Even cars with the most stainless reputations are not expected to last that long, and no Mark I other than those isolated examples which have been little used, or stored for long periods, can be expected to have escaped major deterioration of the bodywork. Buyers of Mark I Sprites, and early Mark IIs and Mark I Midgets, must expect to do a good deal of restorative work, in particular of the floor and rear suspension take-up points.

It is no use disguising the fundamental nature of this work. Restoration of early cars usually means extensive rebuilding of the floor. It is better to tackle this as a whole, as it is not easy to do it patchwork fashion. The structure is already full of seams and joints, because the original tooling was done on a basis of strict economy, which meant lots of small pressings rather than a few large ones. There were over 50 parts from between 21-swg to $\frac{1}{8}$-in plate in the platform, transmission tunnel, cross-members and the fabricated front and rear bulkheads. Simply cutting-out and making-good rusted areas, particularly round the vital suspension pick-ups, may only be postponing the day when a new floor becomes necessary; a good deal depends on how seriously the restoration work is being taken. Do you want the car for Christmas or for life?

Outer sills are adapted by firms such as AH Spares, of Leamington Spa, from the standard BL parts for later models, but the suspension mountings and floor pans of Mark I cars may have to be made in their entirety. This implies professional standards of work, but the reward can be a car in many respects better than new. With the application of modern rustproofing methods and improved paint techniques, a well-restored Sprite could be made to last indefinitely.

Other critical areas which buyers should look at carefully are the door pillars, both around the hinges and where they join the sills. Dirt accumulates inside the sills which, when wet, creates ideal rusting conditions, readily visible as the familiar red blistering on the outside paintwork. The inside rear wheelarches and the areas around the headlights of Mark II and subsequent models are also vulnerable, together with the base of the scuttle panel where it joins the floor pan.

Hoods wear out, but are relatively easy to replace. Trim is also relatively straightforward to remake or renew, with the notable exception of the Mark I floor covering already mentioned. Many Mark Is have had damaged or rusted bonnets replaced with glass-fibre mouldings, which look perfectly acceptable, but for the serious restorer are no substitute for the real thing. The steel bonnet structure, on the other hand, is complicated and expensive to rebuild. A complete bonnet in good condition is not unknown, but is unusual owing to its vulnerability to accident damage. Even quite a small collision crumples it, and bending it straight again without wrinkles is difficult, although less so than dealing with the ravages of rust in the door pillars and the rear bulkhead.

On later models, with bonnets and boots, the bulkhead, door pillar and sills remain rust traps, also the inner rear wheelarches and the rear suspension mountings. Amongst the new body panels, the seams around the front wheelarches, and the rear of the car around the boot floor, where water leaks could be a problem, should all be suspect.

Spridget trim and upholstery is often badly worn because the materials were seldom of a very high quality. As a corollory, however, repair and replacement of upholstery, carpets, or door linings is similarly cheap and easy. Restorers can often make better one-off jobs than the manufacturers ever did, giving the car more luxury and a better level of equipment than it had when new. This is an excusable tendency for the cherished two-seater, even though the concours purists may frown. Most of the problems with the interior arise from the scuffing inevitable in a small, cramped car, together with the ravages which often follow a worn, leaky hood. Accumulations of rain water often contributed to floor pan rust.

Prospective Spridget buyers will usually examine cars for signs of competition use. Evidence of engine tuning can sometimes be obvious, but they will also look for sump guards, painted-over decals and competition numbers, or roll-cage mountings. Roll-cages often play a strong role in maintaining the stiffness of a stripped and lightened body structure, so beware of test drives with the cage in place as a means of detecting rattles and creaks. Wheelarch extensions to accommodate wide tyres should be viewed with apprehension in view of the likely effect they have had on wheel bearings and suspension. Wide wheels themselves may not be at all suitable for the car, no matter how much one feels they may add to the appearance, and that, too, is a matter of taste. Inappropriate wheels and tyres ruin the handling, make the steering heavy and produce no worthwhile improvement in grip. They only serve to wear out transmissions and suspensions prematurely and could even be illegal. Evidence of accident damage or a racy past should be reflected in the price.

Engines are robust on the whole and easy to work on. Some, however, are best avoided, such as those on HAN 7 and GAN 3 cars of 1962-4, the 1,098-cc versions of the Mark II Sprite and Mark I Midget with the rather weak crankshafts. Some of these cars were equipped afterwards with later-series engines. It is possible to ring changes like this on various models, installing different engines to achieve more speed and reliability or, in the case of the 1100s, more smoothness.

Yet if the engines are notably strong, the same may not be said of the transmissions. Clutches tend to have been hard-worked and worn, although replacement with proprietary units is straightforward enough. Noisy first gears and worn synchromesh on second can be more worrisome signs that a major gearbox job is imminent. The gearboxes were rarely quiet when new, but the mangling noises of a defeated first gear are unmistakable.

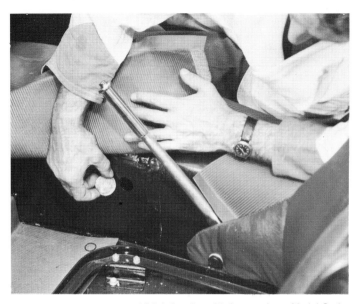

Almost the only accessory which is irreplaceable in restoring a Mark I Sprite is the ribbed, rubbery floor covering. Here, the mat has been lifted to reveal a feature of early models, the access hole for the grease nipple on the propeller-shaft front universal joint.

Likewise, differentials were usually noisy and the nature of the car means the driver hears them distinctly. Accept only a limited amount of free play in the transmission. Half-shaft breakages were common with the stresses imposed by racing tyres.

Looking for accidental damage is important to the buyers of any car, and this is no less true with Spridgets, even those intended for rebuilds. Major damage is often revealed underneath through distortions, and inspection of the underside may also reveal damage sustained during rallies. Modern special-stage events can have a serious effect on bodies.

Rallies are also hard on the suspension. The rear pick-up points have already been mentioned as a source of trouble, particularly on quarter-elliptically sprung cars. But even on quite new cars the dampers wore out relatively quickly, spoiling the taut handling. The A35 front suspension bushes and trunnions are subject to wear, also the steering ball-joint; suspect heavily or unevenly worn tyres as evidence of steering wear.

The brakes are sound and reliable, but they have to work quite hard, not only on account of the heavy use to which the typical Spridget owner will have put them, but also because they are amongst the smallest practical disc brakes. Pads wear quickly and replacement may have been overlooked, making scored discs a strong likelihood. A test drive will reveal any tendency to pull to one side under braking, or even in normal driving. Any such deviation should not be confused with the feel on early cars which the road-testers described as 'nervousness' or 'twitchiness'. It is not even the same as so-called bump-steer. With a light touch on the wheel, a Spridget ought to follow a true, straight course. The steering should be light, and the car responsive to corrections on heavy cambers or over bumps, but it should not wander.

A 1962 survey by *Motor Sport* revealed the trends of Sprite troubles a bare four years after the model's introduction. Perhaps it is an indication of the problems of under-financing and under-development, which were to plague BMC and subsequently BL, that many of the difficulties of the early cars persisted through to the end.

Engine. The biggest problems concerned oil leaks, but since a lot of these were from the oil filter sealing, it must be supposed they were mostly caused by bad fitting during changes, and not by any fundamental failure or shortcoming of the design. Otherwise, most of the troubles were relatively minor or isolated. These, of course, were pre-1,100-cc engines.

Transmission. Quite a lot of clutches were replaced before 18,000 miles, indicating heavy wear in owners' hands, but the main source of criticism was gearbox noise and poor synchromesh. The same went for the rear axle, which already displayed the symptoms of noise and backlash which were to be familiar for many years.

Brakes. Short lining life was the principal source of complaint. Like the clutch, this was the result of heavy use and the saloon-car components not being man enough for the job. The need for constant adjustment and the relining of drums under 20,000 miles was thought to be over-frequent.

Steering and suspension. The rack-and-pinion steering proved almost completely troublefree, but critics of the suspension complained about noise and bottoming. The principal failures were of shock absorbers, but there were several new rear springs as well.

Other defects. Six cars in every 10 had an instrument failure of one sort or another, but the crop of rev-counter drives which seized was probably due to the attachment to the rear of the dynamo being over-tightened. Half the cars in the survey had had some electrical trouble, mostly minor, but listed under bodywork complaints were several cases of water leaks.

Nearly 71 per cent of Sprite owners said they would buy another.

One interesting sidelight of the survey concerned engine modifications. Nearly 20 per cent had replaced the exhaust, which may say something about the life expectation of the standard system, or perhaps the need for self-advertisement by the average owner.

So, which model should be regarded as the Best Buy?

For anyone looking for the most troublefree car, of course, there is no substitute for the newest Spridget they can find. The rubber-bumpered Midgets were neither as pretty, nor handled as well as the earlier models, which rules them out from amongst the most desirable. A great deal depends on how the buyer regards the precision, feel and good balance of the car he drives, and how much he values troublefree motoring in a modern, open two-seater; even the so-called 'soft-nosed' cars are a good deal of fun.

For the dedicated Sprite restorer, the Mark I will remain the *only* Sprite. In good condition, it represents the purest form of Spridget, with all that implies in sensitive handling and wrist-action steering. Enthusiasts for the Mark I claim that from then on the coinage was debased, and that all subsequent Marks are not worth driving. Up to a point they may be right, and there is a supportable 'what if' argument which says that BMC should have had the courage to go on producing the Mark I, as a sort of sporting Volkswagen, more or less indefinitely. They should never have changed it fundamentally, only developed and refined it within its tight design envelope, without adding weight and complication.

This might indeed have resulted in a classic of quite a different sort. Pursuit of the car that might have been could provide a line of research for a Mark I restorer. What about a super-smooth economy 'frog-eye' with the A-Plus Metro engine?

It is also true that as early as the Mark II Sprite handling

The photographer needed to illuminate the gloomy recesses of the luggage area of this Mark I Sprite in order to reveal the spare wheel, which is secured in place by webbing straps. Most owners tended to discard the pvc mat, which soon became dirty. The wiring at the rear is for the stop and tail-lamps.

became less taut, the ride softer and the interior less spartan. It all depends on what degree of creature comfort one demands, and even though luxury is not a term to be applied loosely to the Spridget, how free from discomfort one needs to be.

It follows that nominations for Best Buy must lie somewhere between the Mark I and the 'soft-nosed' cars. Mark II½ Sprites and Mark I½ Midgets are ruled out on account of that wobbly crankshaft. Condition governs the other Marks up to 1974, but of them all, probably the most desirable will be the 1966-74 Marks IV and V Sprite (including the comparatively rare Austin Sprites) and Midgets up to the 1974 GAN 5, with the large fuel tank. The advantages of these cars include the 1,275-cc engine, giving a lively 95 mph and a fuel consumption which, with a certain amount of restraint, could still be on the right side of 30 mpg.

They have all the advantages of the later hoods, although some of the styling changes and wheel forms are matters of taste. None of these considerations represent fundamental shortcomings, however; if you do not like the black windscreen surround, it can be changed. Both pre-winding window and post-winding window cars have their own advantages to consider on their merits, such as weight and elbow-room.

Cars of this era will tend to be dealt with as secondhand vehicles rather than collectors' items. Their handling, although softer than the Mark I's, remains good and they have the good proportions which distinguished all Marks up to 1974.

It is possible to change a rubber-bumpered Spitfire-engined Marina-gearboxed Midget into one that at least looks like the earlier model. The suspension can be lowered and the springs decambered, but the engineering needed to do the job is of an advanced standard. Yet the result would be worthwhile, producing a light, fast, entertaining car with much of the poise and balance of the original.

Whether or not it would be worth the expense is another matter. It might be easier to crop it and tack on the Arkley items, making it into a latter-day Mark I instead. Alternatively, one could start with a floor platform (new or restored as necessary), engine and transmission, rather as the works did, and produce a replica of a Targa Florio car, or a Sebring Sprite, building the appropriate aluminium or plastic body panels to reproduce an authentic period racer.

It all depends on the scope of the workshop, or the depth of the pocket.

APPENDIX A

Technical specifications of all Sprites and Midgets

Austin-Healey Sprite Mark I HAN 5
Engine: BMC A-Type; 4-cyl, 62.94mm (2.478in) × 76.2mm (3.00in), 948cc (57.87cu in); CR 8.3:1 (9.0:1 optional); 2 SU HI 1$\frac{1}{8}$in (28.5mm) carbs; 43bhp (32kW) at 5,200rpm; maximum torque 52lb ft (7.19mkg) at 3,300rpm (high compression); pushrod overhead valves; 3 main crankshaft bearings; Champion N5 plugs; AC mechanical fuel pump; piston area 19.29sq in (124.46sq cm); oil capacity 6$\frac{7}{8}$ pints (3.88 litres) including filter.
Transmission: 6$\frac{1}{4}$in (15.87cm) single-dry-plate clutch; 4-speed gearbox, synchromesh on 2nd 3rd and top; ratios 3.627:1, 2.374:1, 1.412:1, 1.0:1, reverse 4.664:1; final-drive ratio 4.22:1; close-ratio box available with 3.2:1, 1.916:1, 1.357:1, 1.0:1, reverse 4.114:1.
Suspension: Independent front suspension by coil springs and wishbones; lever-arm hydraulic shock absorbers; live rear axle, $\frac{1}{4}$-elliptic 15-leaf springs, radius arms; lever-arm hydraulic shock absorbers.
Chassis: Rack-and-pinion steering, 2$\frac{1}{4}$ turns lock to lock; turning circles 28ft 6in (8.68m) left, 29ft 6in (8.99m) right; Lockheed hydraulic brakes, 7in (17.78cm) drums; mechanical handbrake to rear; tyres 5.20—13in tubeless, 18psi (1.27kg cm) front, 20 psi (1.41kg cm) rear; 13 × 3.5D ventilated steel disc wheels; battery BT7A 43 amp/hr.
Dimensions: Height (hood up) 4ft 1$\frac{3}{4}$in (1.25m); length 11ft 5$\frac{1}{4}$in (3.49m); wheelbase 6ft 8in (2.03m); ground clearance 5in (12.7cm); width 4ft 5in (1.35m); front track 3ft 9$\frac{3}{4}$in (1.16m), rear track 3ft 8$\frac{3}{4}$in (1.14m); fuel capacity 6 gallons (7.2 US gallons) (27.3 litres).
Options: UK May 1958: Heater £20.16.3; radio £25.0.0; tachometer £4.10.0; front bumper and overriders £6.0.0; screenwash £2.5.0; 6-ply tyres £7.2.6; laminated windscreen £4.2.6; fresh-air unit £6.0.0; tonneau cover £6.0.0; UK 1959-60: Hardtop £49.11.8; locking petrol cap £0.17.9. Price reductions followed a lowering of the rate of Purchase Tax.
Prices*: UK May 1958: £455 basic + £233.17.0 Purchase Tax = £678.17.0.
UK 1959-60: £445 basic + £186.10.10 Purchase Tax = £631.10.10.
*Including hood, sidescreens, rear overriders and spare wheel.

Austin-Healey Sprite Mark II HAN 6
MG Midget GAN 1
Engine: BMC A-Type; 4-cyl 62.94mm (2.478in) × 76.2mm (3.00in), 948cc (57.87cu in); CR 9:1 (8.3:1 optional); 2 SU HS2 1$\frac{1}{4}$in (31.75mm) carbs; 46bhp (34.3kW) at 5,500rpm; maximum torque 52.8lb ft (7.3mkg) at 3,000rpm; pushrod overhead valves; 3 main crankshaft bearings; Champion N5 plugs; AC mechanical fuel pump; piston area 19.29sq in (124.46sq cm); oil capacity 6$\frac{7}{8}$ pints (3.88 litres) including filter.
Transmission: 6$\frac{1}{4}$in (15.87cm) single-dry-plate clutch; 4-speed gearbox, synchromesh on 2nd, 3rd and top; ratios 3.2:1, 1.916:1, 1.357:1, 1.0:1,

reverse 4.114:1; final-drive ratio 4.22:1.
Suspension: Independent front suspension by coil springs and wishbones; lever-arm hydraulic shock absorbers; live rear axle, $\frac{1}{4}$-elliptic 15-leaf springs, radius arms; lever-arm hydraulic shock absorbers.
Chassis: Rack-and-pinion steering, 2$\frac{1}{4}$ turns lock to lock; turning circles 32ft 1$\frac{1}{2}$in (9.79m) left, 31ft 2$\frac{1}{2}$in (9.51m) right; Lockheed hydraulic brakes, 7in (17.78cm) drums; mechanical handbrake to rear; tyres 5.20—13in tubeless, 18psi (1.27kg cm) front, 20psi (1.41kg cm) rear; 13 × 3.5D ventilated steel disc wheels; battery BT7A 43 amp/hr.
Dimensions: Height (hood up) 4ft 1$\frac{3}{4}$in (1.25m); length 11ft 5$\frac{7}{8}$in (3.5m); wheelbase 6ft 8in (2.03m); ground clearance 5in (12.7cm); width 4ft 5in (1.35m); front track 3ft 9$\frac{3}{4}$in (1.16m), rear track 3ft 8$\frac{3}{4}$in (1.14m); fuel capacity 6 gallons (7.2 US gallons) (27.3 litres).
Options: UK June 1961: Hardtop £49.11.8 (with sliding sidescreens £69.10.0); heater £17.0.0; radio £29.7.11; heavy-duty tyres £6.7.6; whitewall tyres £7.5.3; laminated windscreen £3.17.11; fresh-air unit £5.13.4; tonneau cover and rail £6.7.6; locking petrol cap £0.17.9; cigar lighter £1.11.2; Ace wheel discs £15.18.9; twin horns £1.11.2; rear seat cushion £4.5.0; luggage carrier and wing mirror £12.7.11; wing mirror only £1.4.10.
Prices*: Austin-Healey Sprite:
UK June 1961: £452 basic + £189.9.2 Purchase Tax = £641.9.2.
UK July 1961: £452 basic + £208.9.6 Purchase Tax = £660.9.6.
*Including front and rear bumpers, overriders, tachometer, windscreen washer and adjustable passenger seat.
MG Midget:
UK June 1961: £472 basic + £187.15.10 = £669.15.10.
UK July 1961: £472 basic + £217.11.5 = £689.11.5.
USA prices: Suggested United States retail prices, East, West, and Gulf Coasts Ports of Entry (including US Customs duties and Federal Excise Tax, but excluding inland freight, local and State taxes where applicable):
March 1961: $1795.00.
Options: Heater $60.00; screenwash $15.00; tachometer $30.00; tonneau cover and rail $25.00; whitewall tyres $30.00; hardtop $179.00; tuning conditions 1-5, $340.00.

Austin-Healey Sprite Mark II 1100 HAN 7
MG Midget 1100 GAN 2
Engine: BMC A-Type; 4-cyl, 64.58mm (2.543in) × 83.72mm (3.296in), 1,098cc (66.99cu in); CR 8.9:1 (8.1:1 optional); 2 SU HS2 1$\frac{1}{4}$in (31.75mm) carbs; 56bhp (41.7kW) at 5,500rpm; maximum torque 62lb ft (8.6mkg) at 3,250rpm (high compression); pushrod overhead valves; 3 main crankshaft bearings; Champion N5 plugs; AC mechanical fuel pump; piston area

20.3sq in (130.97sq cm); oil capacity 6 ½ pints (3.7 litres).

Transmission: 7¼in (18.4cm) single-dry-plate clutch, 4-speed gearbox, synchromesh on 2nd, 3rd and top; ratios 3.2:1, 1.916:1, 1.357:1, 1.0:1, reverse 4.120:1; final-drive ratio 4.22:1.

Suspension: Independent front suspension by coil springs and wishbones; lever-arm hydraulic shock absorbers; live rear axle, ¼-elliptic 15-leaf springs, radius arms; lever-arm hydraulic shock absorbers.

Chassis: Rack-and-pinion steering, 2¼ turns lock to lock; turning circles 32ft 1½in (9.79m) left, 31ft 2½in (9.51m) right; Lockheed hydraulic brakes, disc front, drum rear, 8¼in (20.9cm) discs, 7in (17.8cm) drums; mechanical handbrake to rear; tyres 5.20—13in tubeless, 18psi (1.27kg cm) front, 20psi (1.41kg cm) rear; 13 × 3.5D pressed-steel disc wheels; battery N9 or N29 43 amp/hr.

Dimensions: Height (hood up) 4ft 1¾in (1.25m); length 11ft 5⅝in (3.5m); wheelbase 6ft 8in (2.03m); ground clearance 5in (12.7cm); width 4ft 5in (1.35m); front track 3ft 9¼in (1.16m); rear track 3ft 8¾in (1.14m); fuel capacity 6 gallons (7.2 US gallons) (27.3 litres).

Options: Radio; heater; tonneau cover; laminated windscreen; hardtop; cigar lighter; heavy-duty tyres; twin horns; luggage carrier; rear seat cushion.

Prices: UK 1962-63: Sprite: £485 basic + £101.12.0 Purchase Tax = £586.12.0.

Midget: £495 basic + £103.13.9 Purchase Tax = £598.13.9.

Austin-Healey Sprite Mark III HAN 8
MG Midget Mark II GAN 3

Engine: BMC A-Type; 4-cyl; 64.58mm (2.543in) × 83.72mm (3.296in), 1,098cc (66.99cu in); CR 8.9:1 (9.1:1 optional); 2 SU HS2 1¼in (31.75mm) carbs; 59bhp (43.99kW) at 5,750rpm; maximum torque 65lb ft (8.9mkg) at 3,500rpm; pushrod overhead valves; 3 main crankshaft bearings; Champion N5 plugs; SU electric fuel pump; piston area 20.3sq in (130.97sq cm); oil capacity 6 ½ pints (3.7 litres).

Transmission: 7¼in (18.4cm) single-dry-plate clutch; 4-seed gearbox, synchromesh on 2nd, 3rd and top; ratios 3.2:1, 1.916:1, 1.357:1, 1.0:1, reverse 4.120:1; final-drive ratio 4.22:1.

Suspension: Independent front suspension by coil springs and wishbones; lever-arm hydraulic shock absorbers; live rear axle, ½-elliptic, 5-leaf springs; lever-arm hydraulic shock absorbers.

Chassis: Rack-and-pinion steering, 2¼ turns lock to lock; turning circles 32ft 1½in (9.79m) left, 31ft 2½in (9.51m) right; Lockheed hydraulic brakes, disc front, drum rear, 8¼in (20.9cm) discs, 7in (17.8cm) drums; mechanical handbrake to rear; tyres 5.20—13in tubeless, 18psi (1.27kg cm) front, 20psi (1.41kg cm) rear; 13 × 3.5D pressed-steel disc wheels; battery N9 or N29 43 amp/hr.

Dimensions: Height (hood up) 4ft 1¾in (1.25m); length 11ft 5⅝in (3.5m); wheelbase 6ft 8in (2.03m); ground clearance 5in (12.7cm); width 4ft 5in (1.35m); front track 3ft 9¼in (1.16m), rear track 3ft 8¾in (1.14m); fuel capacity 6 gallons (7.2 US gallons) (27.3 litres).

Options: Radiomobile radio; heater; hardtop; luggage carrier; twin horns.

heavy-duty tyres; wheel discs; tonneau cover.

Prices: UK 1964-66:

Sprite: £505 basic + £105.15.5 Purchase Tax = £610.15.5.

Midget: £515 basic + £107.17.1 Purchase Tax = £622.17.1.

USA:

Sprite: $1925. Midget: $2095.

Austin-Healey Sprite Mark IV HAN 9
MG Midget Mark III GAN 4
Austin-Healey Sprite Mark V HAN 10
MG Midget Mark IV GAN 5
Austin Sprite AAN 10

Engine: BMC Cooper S; 4-cyl; 70.61mm (2.78in) × 81.28mm (3.2in), 1,275cc (77.8cu in); compression ratio 8.8:1 (8.0:1 optional); 2 SU HS2 1¼in carbs; 65bhp (48.47kW) at 6,000rpm; maximum torque 72lb ft (9.96mkg) at 3,000rpm (high compression); pushrod overhead valves; 3 main crankshaft bearings; Champion N9Y plugs; SU electric fuel pump; piston area 24.28sq in (156.63sq cm); oil capacity 6 ½ pints (3.7 litres).

Transmission: 6½in (165mm) diaphragm-spring clutch; 4-speed gearbox, synchromesh on 2nd, 3rd and top; ratios 3.2:1, 1.916:1, 1.357:1, 1.0:1, reverse 4.114:1; final-drive ratio 4.22:1; 3.9:1 from Sprite 77573.

Suspension: Independent front suspension by coil springs and wishbones; lever-arm hydraulic shock absorbers; live rear axle, ½-elliptic 5-leaf springs; lever-arm hydraulic shock absorbers.

Chassis: Rack-and-pinion steering, 2¼ turns lock to lock; turning circle 32ft 1½in (9.79m) left, 31ft 2½in (9.51m) right; Lockheed hydraulic brakes, disc front, drum rear, 8¼in (20.9cm) discs, 7in (17.8cm) drums; mechanical handbrake to rear; tyres 5.20—13in cross-ply, 145SR—13in radial-ply; wheels 4½JSL × 13 pressed-steel spoked; 3.5D × 13 pressed-steel disc, 4J × 13 wire; tyre pressures 18psi (1.27kg cm) front cross-ply, 20psi (1.4kg cm) rear cross-ply; 22psi (1.55kg cm) front radial, 24psi (1.69kg cm) rear radial; battery A9/AZ9 — A11/AZ11 40 or 50 amp/hr.

Dimensions: Height (hood up) 4ft 1¾in (1.25m); length 11ft 5½in (3.5m); wheelbase 6ft 8in (2.03m); ground clearance 5in (12.7cm); width 4ft 5in (1.35m); front track 3ft 9¼in (1.16m), rear track 3ft 8¾in (1.14m); fuel capacity 6 gallons (7.2 US gallons) (27.3 litres).

Options: Heater; radio; seat belts; tonneau cover; hardtop.

Prices: UK 1966-67:

Sprite: £545 basic + £127 Purchase Tax = £672.

Midget: £555 basic + £129 Purchase Tax = £684.

MG Midget GAN 6 (Mark nomenclature no longer valid)

Engine: Triumph, 4-cyl; 73.7mm (2.9in) × 87.5mm (3.44in), 1,493cc (91.1cu in); CR 9.0:1; 2 SU HS4 1½in (38.1mm) carbs; 66bhp (49.22kW) at 5,500rpm; maximum torque 77lb ft (10.64mkg) at 3,000rpm; pushrod overhead valves; 3 main crankshaft bearings; Champion N9Y plugs; SU mechanical fuel pump; piston area 26.44sq in (170.63sq cm); oil capacity 8 pints (4.5 litres).

Transmission: 7¼in (18.4cm) diaphragm-spring clutch; 4-speed, all-synchromesh gearbox; ratios 3.41:1, 2.11:1, 1.43:1, 1.0:1, reverse 3.75:1; final-drive ratio 3.9:1.
Suspension: Independent front suspension by coil springs and wishbones; lever-arm shock absorbers; anti-roll bar; live rear axle, ½-elliptic 6-leaf springs; lever-arm hydraulic shock absorbers.
Chassis: Rack-and-pinion steering, 2¾ turns lock to lock; turning circles 30ft 10in (9.39m) left, 31ft 11in (9.72m) right; Lockheed hydraulic brakes, disc front, drum rear, 8¼in (20.9cm) discs, 7in (17.8cm) drums; mechanical handbrake; tyres 145–13in radial-ply, 22psi (1.55kg cm) front, 24 psi (1.69kg cm) rear; battery 40 amp/hr.

Dimensions: Height (hood up) 4ft 0½in (1.23m); length 11ft 9in (3.58m); wheelbase 6ft 8in (2.03m); ground clearance 5in (12.7cm); width 4ft 5½in (1.36m); front track 3ft 10½in (1.18m), rear track 3ft 9in (1.14m); fuel capacity 7 gallons (8.4 US gallons) (31.8 litres).
Options: Wire wheels; hardtop.
Prices: UK 1975:
£1333.00 basic, Special Car Tax £111.08 + VAT £115.53 = £1,559.61. During the currency of this model the price was subject to frequent change and rose to £3,821 by the time production came to an end. US specifications diverged owing to emission-control and other regulations, and a number of special options were included in US cars from time to time.

APPENDIX B
Sprite and Midget identification reference

Austin-Healey Sprite
Announcement May 20, 1958. Production started March 31, 1958.
Design reference ADO 13.
Chassis prefix AN5.
In production 1958-61.
Original 'frog-eyed' Sprite; Morris Minor 948-cc, 43-bhp engine; ¼-elliptic rear springs; lift-up bonnet and front wings in one piece; no external boot access; lightweight sidescreens; hood-to-windscreen fixing modified after Chassis Number 5477, October 16, 1958.·

Austin-Healey Sprite Mark II
Announcement May 1961.
Design reference ADO 41.
Chassis prefix AN6.

MG Midget
Announcement June 1961.
Design reference ADO 47.
Chassis prefix AN1.
In production 1961-2.
Second-generation Sprite and first Midget; restyled front and rear; more power from 948-cc engine; close-ratio gearbox standard; conventional bonnet and boot-lid; ¼-elliptic rear springs remain; MG version with vertically slatted grille, chrome side strips, superior seats and flecked rubber floor trim.

Austin-Healey Sprite Mark II ('1100')
Announcement October 1962.
Chassis prefix AN7.

MG Midget ('1100')
Announcement October 1962.
Chassis prefix AN2.
In production 1962-4.
Simultaneous announcement of two models for London Motor Show; 1,098-cc engine; disc brakes; baulk-ring synchromesh; carpets and improved trim; padded roll on facia; sliding sidescreens; ¼-elliptic rear springs remain.

Austin-Healey Sprite Mark III
Announcement March 1964.
Chassis prefix AN8.

MG Midget Mark II
Announcement March 1964.
Chassis prefix AN3.
In production 1964-6.
Restyling including winding windows and new windscreen; lockable doors; facia instruments angled towards driver; black crackle dashboard finish; improved trim; MG 1100 cylinder-head, more power; rear springs changed to ½-elliptics.

Austin-Healey Sprite Mark IV
Announcement October 1966.
Chassis prefix AN9.

MG Midget Mark III
Announcement October 1966.
Chassis prefix AN4.
In production 1966-9.

Announced for London Motor Show; unchanged externally but fitted with detuned Mini-Cooper S 1275 engine; hood fixed to rear deck; larger cockpit opening.

Austin-Healey Sprite Mark V
Announcement October 1969.
Chassis prefix AN10.

Austin Sprite
Announcement January 1971.
Chassis prefix AAN10.

MG Midget Mark IV
Announcement October 1969.
Chassis prefix AN5.

In production 1969-71 (Sprite), 1969-74 (Midget).
Minor styling changes; oval common grille for both models; black sills and windscreen surround; rounded rear wheelarch; Rostyle wheels. Modifications from October 1970: improved heater; lights for boot and interior; automatic boot and bonnet stays; larger fuel tank; rear wheelarch squared-off again; collapsible steering column.

MG Midget Mark IV 1500
Announcement October 1974.
Chassis prefix AN6.
In production 1974-9.
Triumph Spitfire engine; Morris Marina gearbox; soft bumpers; various detail modifications to suit different market requirements. Last car built November 1979.

APPENDIX C

Chassis and Engine Number reference

Sprite identification data

Model		Starting		Finishing
H-AN5	engine	9C/U/H101		9C/U/H49201
	chassis	H-AN5-501		H-AN5-50116
H-AN6	engine	9CGDa/H101		9CGDa/H36711
and	or	9CGDa/L	or	9CGDa/L
H-AN7	or	10CG 101	or	10CG 21048
Mk II	chassis	H-AN6-101		H-AN6-24731
		H-AN7-24732		H-AN7-38828
H-AN8	engine	10CC/Da/H101		10CC/Da/H16300
Mk III	chassis	H-AN8-38829		H-AN8-64734
H-AN9	engine	12CC/Da/H101		12CC/Da/H16300
and		12CE/Da/H101		
H-AN10		12CG/Da/H101		
and				
A-AN10	chassis	H-AN9-64735		H-AN9-85286
Mk IV		H-AN10-85287		H-AN10-86803
		A-AN10-86804		A-AN10-87824

Sprite Chassis Numbers
First Chassis Number in January 1971 was 86803.
First Austin Sprite A-AN10 was 86804.
Last Sprite made in July 1971 was 87824.
Production of Austin Sprites was 1,022, suggesting that they ran from Chassis Numbers 86803 to 87824 without breaks. The official BL parts list quotes the first Austin-Healey Sprite as 86403, but it must be concluded that this is a misprint and should have been 86803.

Midget identification data

Model		Starting		Finishing
G-AN1	engine	9CGDa/H101		9CGDa/H36711
Mk I	or	9CGDa/L	or	9CGDa/L
and	or	10CG 101	or	10CG 21048
G-AN2				
	chassis	G-AN1-101		G-AN1-16183
		G-AN2-16184		G-AN2-25787
G-AN3	engine	10CC/Da/H101		10CC/Da/H16300
Mk II	chassis	G-AN3-25788		G-AN3-52389
G-AN4	engine	12CC/Da/H101		12CC/Da/H16300

Model		Starting	Finishing
G-AN5		12CD/Da/H101	not available
Mk III		12CE/Da/H101	
Mk IV	USA	12CF/Da/H101	
	USA	12CG/Da/H101	
	USA	12CH/Da/H101	
	USA	12CJ/Da/H21201	
	USA	12CK/Da/H101	
		12V/586F/101	
	USA	12V/587Z/101	
		12V/588F/101	
	chassis	G-AN4-52390	G-AN4-74885
		G-AN5-74886	G-AN5-153920
G-AN6	engine	FP-001-E	79144
	engine USA	FP-300-UE	79141
	engine Calif.	FP-400-UCE	
	chassis	G-AN6-154101	G-AN6-229526
	body (UK)	GB47T 040001 P	GB47T 954383 P
	body (USA)	GU47T 004001 P	

Midget Chassis Numbers by calendar year 1971 to 1979

	Starting No.	Number made
1971	96853	16410
1972	113617	16158
1973	129861	14130
1974	144038	12449
1975	156667	14502
1976	171356	17121
1977	188814	14340
1978	204350	15400
1979	219750	9777

Midget Chassis Numbers by model year 1970 to 1980

	Prefix			Number made
1970	G-AN5-UA	from	75715 to 88596	12882
1971	G-AN5-UB	from	89501 to 105146	15646
1972	G-AN5-UC	from	105501 to 123644	18144
1973	G-AN5-UD	from	123731 to 138753	15023
1974	G-AN5-UE	from	138801 to 153920	15120
1975	G-AN6-UF	from	154101 to 166193	12093
1976	G-AN6-UG	from	166301 to 181663	15363
1977	G-AN6-UH	from	182001 to 198804	16804
1978	G-AN6-UJ	from	200001 to 212393	12393
1979	G-AN6-UL	from	212394 to 229000	16607
1980	G-AN6-UM	from	229001 to 229526	526

Letter U is found on North American-specification cars, indicating USA, followed by a letter A to M, indicating model year, which is also found only on North American vehicles. The 1980 model-year cars suffixed M were exported only to Canada, not to the USA.

It is not certain if 229000/1 actually indicates the split between the 1979 and 1980 model years. Of those cars built with numbers higher than 229000, 229001 to 229500 were black and all were supplied to the home market. The final car, numbered 229526, was also black and went to BL Heritage. It is featured on the cover of this book. Cars numbered 229501 to 229525 are believed to have been exported, possibly to Japan.

Notes on tables

Serial number prefix code:
First letter: name — G = MG, H = Austin-Healey, A = Austin
Second letter: engine type — A = A-series, including 1500 cars
Third letter: body type — N = two-seat tourer
Fourth number: series of model — 6 = sixth series of MG Midget
Fifth letter: if not rhd — either L = lhd or U = USA
Sixth letter: model year — USA and Canada cars only, following U.

Model years: The changeover normally occurred in August or September, *eg,* the 1975 model year ran from August 1974 to August 1975, but the dates were dependent upon model changeovers and the timing of holiday breaks.

All Sprites and Midgets were assembled at Abingdon with the exception of 489 AN9 Sprites and 476 AN4 Midgets built at Cowley between January and March 1967. They may be identified with an M suffix.

There is no correlation between Chassis Numbers (more properly, Car Numbers) and Engine Numbers or Body Numbers. For example, the first Mark I Sprite chassis was numbered H-AN5-501, and the first engine 9C/U/H101, but the two never met. Engine Number 101 actually went into Chassis Number 732, while Chassis Number 501 had Engine Number 173, probably because it happened to be the first off the lorry from Morris Engines. Similarly, the first chassis had Body Number 630, the second 622 and the third 508.

Research on the numbers of cars made and their identification numbers was carried out in collaboration with Anders Clausager, BL Heritage archivist, without whom it would have been an almost impossible task. The company records do not maintain running totals, which have led earlier researchers to conclude some slightly different figures from those given here. There has been some uncertainty about the number of Austin Sprites built after the Healey name ran out, for example. From examination of the latest Abingdon records it can be established that 1,022 were manufactured. These match the Chassis Numbers 86803 to 87824, although simply adding and subtracting Chassis Numbers is not always an accurate guide to production owing to deletions or omissions.

It is not known why Cowley was employed to build Spridgets in 1967. It may be surmised, however, that the run-out of the big Austin-Healey and its replacement by the MGC created a certain hiatus at Abingdon at the time. The Chassis Numbers were in the following batches:

Austin-Healey Sprite		MG Midget	
65472 – 65496	25 cars	53352 – 53376	25 cars
65641 – 65727	87	53473 – 53600	128
65944 – 66092	149	53643 – 53697	55
66195 – 66264	70	53754 – 53780	27
66365 – 66434	70	53931 – 54001	71
66585 – 66654	70	54151 – 54217	67
66804 – 66820	17	54353 – 54454	102
67193	1*	54611	1
total	489 cars	total	476 cars

The following batches of Chassis Numbers were allocated to Cowley-built Sprites, but never used:

66821 – 66858	38
67017 – 67096	80
67194 – 67265	72

This means that 190 numbers remained unused. Adding these to the total of 489 Sprites actually built at Cowley comes suspiciously close to the figure of 659 which Abingdon production control has traditionally given.

* The last Cowley-built Sprite was despatched to Donald Healey Motors, at Warwick, but the records do not reveal why.

APPENDIX D

Sprite and Midget production statistics

Total manufacture

Year		Sprite		Midget	Combined	Year
1958	H-AN5	8729			8729	1958
1959		21566			21566	1959
1960		18665			18665	1960
1961		39				
1961	H-AN6	10020	G-AN1	7656	17715	1961
1962		10430		8424		
1962	H-AN7	1611	G-AN2	1482	21947	1962
1963		8852		7625	16477	1963
1964		752		494		
1964	H-AN8	10405	G-AN3	10956	22607	1964
1965		8882		9162	18044	1965
1966		6618		6483		
1966	H-AN9	406	G-AN4	359	13866	1966
1967		6895		8330	15225	1967
1968		7049		5033		
1968			G-AN5	2339	14421	1968
1969	H-AN10	6129		13085	19214	1969
1970		1292		14811	16103	1970
1971	A-AN10	1022		16410	17432	1971
1972				16158	16158	1972
1973				14130	14130	1973
1974				9690		
1974			G-AN6	2759	12449	1974

Year	Sprite	Midget	Combined	Year
1975		14502	14502	1975
1976		17121	17121	1976
1977		14340	14340	1977
1978		15400	15400	1978
1979		9777	9777	1979
total	129362	226526	355888	

	Sprite		Midget
H-AN5	48999	G-AN1	16080
H-AN6	20450	G-AN2	9601
H-AN7	11215	G-AN3	26601
H-AN8	25905	G-AN4	13722
H-AN9	14350	G-AN5	86623
H-AN10	7421	G-AN6	73899
A-AN10	1022		
	129362		226526

APPENDIX E

How fast? How economical? Performance figures model by model

	Sprite I HAN 5	Midget GAN 1 Sprite II HAN 6	Midget GAN 2 Sprite II HAN 7	Midget II GAN 3 Sprite III HAN 8	Midget III GAN 4 Sprite IV HAN 9	Midget IV GAN 5 Sprite V AAN 10	Midget GAN 6
Max speed mph	86.5	85.8	88.6	91.8	93.5	94.0	101
Acceleration (sec)							
0-30 mph	5.1	5.3	4.7	4.2	4.6	4.2	3.7
0-40 mph	8.5	8.6	7.9	6.9	7.0	6.5	5.8
0-50 mph	13.7	13.2	11.5	9.8	9.9	9.6	8.5
0-60 mph	20.5	20.0	16.9	14.7	14.6	14.1	12.3
0-70 mph	31.1	29.9	25.6	20.5	20.7	20.0	17.0
0-80 mph		50.3	37.6	33.9	33.2	29.7	24.0
0-90 mph						51.3	35.3
Overall mpg	33.6	38.6	29.9	29.4	28.4	29.6	27.9
Touring or DIN mpg	43.0	43.5	37.2	30.0 (DIN)	28.8 (DIN)	32.5 (DIN)	32.5 (DIN)
Mpg constant 50 mph	53.5	49.5	44.0	44.0	40.0	55.0	39.2
Mpg constant 70 mph	36.0	39.0	35.5	34.0	31.5	35.5	29.8
Standing ¼-mile (sec)	21.8	22.0	21.0	19.75	19.7	19.6	18.5
Mph/1,000 rpm in top	15.37	15.37	15.37	15.37	15.37	16.44	16.44
Max in 1st (mph)	25.0	29.0	30.0	30.0	30.0	33.0	29.0
Max in 2nd	39.0	48.0	50.0	50.0	50.0	55.0	47.0
Max in 3rd	65.0	67.0	70.0	70.0	70.0	78.0	69.0

Sources for this data include contemporary road tests conducted by *Motor* and *Autocar*